THE PERFECT KEG

The PERF

SOWING, SCYTHING, *and*

to the BEST-EVER

MALTING
BREWING MY WAY
PINT OF BEER

IAN COUTTS

GREYSTONE BOOKS
VANCOUVER/BERKELEY

In memory of Millie, the mash-eating wonder dog

14 15 16 17 18 5 4 3 2 1

Greystone Books Ltd.
www.greystonebooks.com

Cataloguing data available from Library and Archives Canada
ISBN 978-1-77100-008-6 (pbk.)
ISBN 978-1-77100-009-3 (epub)

Editing by Shirarose Wilensky
Copy editing by Maureen Nicholson
Cover and text design by Ingrid Paulson
Cover illustration by Ingrid Paulson
Printed and bound in Canada by Friesens
Distributed in the U.S. by Publishers Group West

We gratefully acknowledge the financial support of the Canada Council for the Arts, the British Columbia Arts Council, the Province of British Columbia through the Book Publishing Tax Credit and the Government of Canada through the Canada Book Fund for our publishing activities.

Greystone Books is committed to reducing the consumption of old-growth forests in the books it publishes. This book is one step toward that goal.

Contents

Introduction

WHEN AMBITION MEETS IGNORANCE

"WHAT ARE YOUR beer ambitions?"

The question brought me up short.

I was part of a panel at Café C'est What?, advertised as a question and answer session with some of the country's top beer writers, for Toronto Beer Week. Nine guys seated on a small stage in a cozy amber and beige cellar bar. The audience, scattered around the room at low tables or propping up a bar boasting more beer pumps than I had ever seen, wrote questions on little pieces of paper and then handed them over to the master of ceremonies, who then read them out to us. The evening had started out with fairly straightforward queries eliciting our thoughts on beer and brewing trends, but it had grown progressively rowdier and more creative as audience and panel swallowed more and more of the evening's subject matter.

Leading to the question about our beer ambitions. Good God. What were my beer ambitions? I don't really associate beer with ambition. Usually they work at cross-purposes. But after thinking about it for a moment, I answered. "Get good at making it." From there we moved on to a discussion of beer's aphrodisiac qualities.

Beer is one of the oldest alcoholic beverages on earth, maybe the oldest. Some historians even think it spurred the birth of civilization. When our hunting and gathering ancestors stumbled on beer, through some lucky accident, they quickly realized that if they wanted more, they were going to have to settle down and get busy inventing farming and brewing. Beer is the most popular alcoholic beverage on earth, and the third most popular drink in the world after water and tea. Traditionally a humble working-man's beverage, beer has come up socially in the past few decades. Today beer fans discuss a particular brew's nose or its finish the way wine snobs talk about a specific vintage. Restaurants offer menus built around pairing beer and food. Some even have a beer sommelier ready to guide your drinking choices among different ales or suggest an amusing wit beer to go with dessert. That sommelier likely studied to become a cicerone, a certified beer expert. Beer festivals and events like the one I was part of attract thousands of people. Never, in living human memory, have there been so many different kinds of beer available to the lucky drinker.

For all that, though, what do we really know about beer? About how it's made, and what it really is? Nowhere, except perhaps Germany, are brewers even obliged to tell you the ingredients in their product. Plenty of beer companies boast about their product's all-natural ingredients, but all-natural what? Too often, when you hold a bottle of beer in your hand, you hold a mystery. I like to think I know a lot about beer. I can explain the difference between ale and lager yeast. I know what makes pale ale pale and imperial stout imperial. I can rattle off the stages of brewing, too. Having said that, if I am honest, I am aware of how little I know.

IN THE WEEKS after that night, I kept thinking about that question and my answer. But just thinking, nothing more. Then one afternoon, my wife, Catharine, and I were out for a walk with Millie, our small black Lab–Mexican street dog. We were visiting the farm she (Catharine, not Millie) co-owns with a bunch of other people in the Ottawa Valley. It was late fall. The leaves were gone and the grass was brown. We trudged down into the lower fields in the direction of the derelict 1940s-era Ford that marks the end of our property. As we walked, with Millie busily trotting ahead of us, we talked about the brewing idea. I'd written about beer and read a lot on it. I'd drunk plenty of it in my time, too. I'd even tried making it over the years, with varying degrees of success, at home and at "you-brew" establishments. Getting really good at making it seemed like a fun next step.

Then it hit me. "Why not do it here?" I said to her. "Make it a whole hundred mile thing. Actually, we could make it a forty acre thing." It was coming to me. "We could plant some barley there," I said, pointing to a sunny patch on the side of a hill. "And run the hops up the side of the chicken coop." I was walking faster. "We've already got fantastic well water." By this point, I was almost running, eager to greet the great future appearing before me: a lifetime supply of beer. And all I had to do was plant it, brew it, bottle it and drink it.

Brewing beer, I realized, would also be a good way to learn more about it—and writing would be a great way to share it with other people. An adventure was starting to take shape. This wouldn't all be me down on the farm, becoming one with the soil and extracting nature's bounty. I'd talk to agronomists and biologists to understand beer at its most fundamental level. I'd work alongside top brewmasters in different breweries to learn the tricks of their craft. I'd visit barley and hop growers. I'd discover how firkins are made. I'd even learn what a firkin is.

In the end I would have a compact little barrel filled with homemade ale. The product of a particular patch of Ontario farmland and a particular time, the second decade of the twenty-first century. But my beer would also be the story of all beer—wherever it is drunk and whenever people have drunk it. I'd know why beer is both bitter and sweet, why German beer tastes German, and British beer, British. I'd understand malting. And I'd know where people got the idea of germinating barley in the first place. IBUs and AAUs, specific gravity, the tasting spectrum—you name it, I'd know it. That mystery in the beer drinker's glass wouldn't be a mystery anymore. I'd gain a deep understanding and appreciation of the science and art of beer—all from brewing one perfect little keg.

"YOU LOOK LIKE BARLEY PEOPLE"

THE SCENE WAS like a bizarre remake of Hitchcock's *Psycho*. *Psycho,* that is, with my wife and me taking over Anthony Perkins's role and a bulky twenty-three-liter plastic bag of ale wort, the sticky, sweet fluid made by steeping crushed barley, standing in for Janet Leigh. We were supposed to pour the sticky brown fluid into a large plastic bin, which we had put in the old clawfoot bathtub of our Kingston house in case we spilled anything. Grunting and bickering, we had wrestled the bag onto the edge of the tub, pushed aside the shower curtain, and then tipped its spout over the plastic bin. Nothing. The spout would not spout. Grabbing a knife, we quickly poked a hole in the bag. A trickle. At this rate we'd be holding the heavy bag in place for half an hour. So we gave it the full Norman Bates. We stabbed the bag again. And again. And again. Soon the sticky brown liquid was flowing into the bin from half a dozen holes, and into the bathtub and onto us. All that was missing were the screeching violins.

Not the most auspicious start. Here we were, undertaking the brewing equivalent of the bunny hill in skiing—we'd bought a beer kit at our local beer and wine supply place, a bag filled with five-plus gallons of wort and a little packet of yeast. All we had to do was get the wort into the tub, then toss in the yeast. And we were already in way over our heads. Couldn't organize a piss-up in a brewery? We couldn't organize brewing in a brewery.

AFTER MY INITIAL inspiration, I'd left the idea of creating the perfect keg alone. Perhaps I hoped that, undisturbed in the quiet and darkness of my head, my idea would mellow and mature, rather like a fine English ale inside a wooden cask. By late winter, however, it was clear that, left to its own devices, the idea had developed all the richness of Coors Light. I had to get going.

Brewing great beer from scratch was going to mean learning two different jobs. First off, there would be Ian the brewmaster. I hadn't brewed beer at home in more than thirty years and when I had, the "brewing" hadn't amounted to much more than dumping a can of syrupy malt extract into a pot of boiling water. Our first recent attempt at brewing—the great bathtub massacre, as I thought of it—

had actually worked out quite well, despite the personal hysteria we managed to inject into the process. It would have been quite hard to ruin our brew, working from a kit, of course. Not that I would have minded if we had—if we'd later been able to work out why. This was about learning. (And besides, no one ever died from drinking bad beer.)

This first brew and the several to follow were about learning to brew properly, to go at it in a systematic way. If we could learn to follow the simple steps needed to make beer starting from a kit, we could build on that and make progressively more complex brews, leading up to that final brew. The thing I realized early on about creating my perfect keg was that I didn't need to wait until I had my raw ingredients before I started brewing. In fact, I shouldn't. I could buy malt and hops and yeast, and equipment, and start learning to brew before I even had a seed in the ground. While everything was germinating or sprouting, I could get better and better at making beer. When my barley and my hops were ready, I would be, too. It'd be like hitting a baseball over your house, going inside, cutting out the leather and stitching together a glove, walking out the front door—and seeing the ball drop into your hand. Just-in-time brewing.

Before we go any further, I need to digress a little to tell you about the ingredients in beer. This is a simplification, but at heart, beer comes down to four things: water, yeast, barley and hops. Fairly simple. But like the blues, another devilishly simple thing, with various tweaks and additions these base ingredients can give rise to an infinite series of variations.

Given how open-ended beer making is, it's not surprising that there was plenty about brewing I didn't know. But in the parlance of Donald Rumsfeld, these gaps were known unknowns—I knew that you had to put some hops into your brew at the beginning and other hops in at the end, I knew that you boiled the wort for an hour when making beer, even if I wasn't sure what kinds of hops or why exactly you boiled it for an hour.

With my other job, farming, I was on shakier footing. It's not that I wasn't aware that I was ignorant. I knew that. But I didn't know what I didn't know.

Well, I did know a couple of things. I knew I was going to need to plant hops and barley. For the hops, I had picked three different varieties out of a nursery catalogue—Cascade, Willamette and Nugget. Hops, for the uninitiated, are what give beer its bitter taste. Generally, that is. There are other factors at play. And with hops, again very generally, the more hops you use, the bitterer your beer will taste. But not all hops are the same; some are naturally more bitter than others. Brewers define hops in terms of their alpha acid content, which is a measure of their bitterness, known as AAUS. Amateur brewers use a slightly different system to describe the same thing—international bittering units, or IBUS.

Hops are about more than bitterness, however; they can also bring specific fragrances to the brew. Cascade hops are characterized by fruity and citrus-like aromas. Cascade is an all-rounder that has become popular in recent years in bitter so-called West Coast–style pale ales. (The Cascade in their name refers to the Cascade Mountains, where they were developed in the 1950s. Most hops grown in North America come from the Pacific Northwest.) In terms of bitterness, Willamette is in the midrange along with Cascade. It is related to the classic British hop with the wonderful name Fuggles. Certain hops work in certain kinds of beer: Willamette would do in a more traditional British-style ale; Nugget might work when you wanted a far more bitter taste.

I chose three kinds of hops in part because I wasn't sure yet what kind of beer I wanted to brew. I had some ideas, but I didn't want to be nailed down so early in the project. I had another reason for mixing my hops. What I was doing was the hop grower's equivalent of laying off side bets. I didn't know what would work best with my soil and weather conditions. If one strain of hop pooped out completely, the other two might pull through.

The flavors and aromas that hops bring to beer are so taken for granted today that it is sometimes hard to believe beer wasn't always made with them. Historically, brewers used just water, malt and yeast—although for a good deal of history, people weren't sure what yeast was. (I'll return to it later.) This brew was prone to going bad quite quickly, ruined by bacteria called *Acetobacter,* which turned the beer to vinegar about as fast as the yeast could ferment it. Beer was by turns sickly sweet or sour, so people fooled around with a lot of different "additives" for beer to improve its flavor, including plants such as juniper and heather. At some point in the ninth century, some German monks experimentally added the flowers from a hop plant to one of their brews and made an exciting discovery—as well as giving the beer an interesting bitter flavor, the hop plants stopped the beer from going off. The use of hops in beer spread across Europe, though slowly, reaching England sometime in the fifteenth century. The parts of the hop you use to flavor beer resemble tiny, soft, pale green pine cones (they are in fact called cones). They have a pungent oiliness to them so that, when you encounter it in freshly picked hops, you seem to both smell and taste at the same time. The hop plant is a cousin of marijuana, and like marijuana there are male and female plants. The ones needed for brewing are the females—the males do flower, but they don't produce the cones.

Not so very long ago, it was hard to order brewing hops from nurseries. Richters, the big herb nursery I ordered from, only started carrying them in the late 1990s. You could get medicinal and ornamental hops—which make a nice trailing vine—but Richters didn't carry even the more common brewing varieties. Now I had my choice of a number of beer-worthy varieties, a result of the boom in home brewing in the past few years. I ordered three of each of variety that I had selected—which was another nice thing about dealing with Richters. Places catering to commercial growers set minimum orders in the dozens. And they would ship roots, not the more developed plants Richters could supply.

Barley was a little more complicated. I knew there were two varieties of barley generally used in making beer—six row and two row. The rows in this case refer not to how they are planted (my original guess) but to how the barley kernels are arranged on the husk. If you look at stalks from the mature plant, you can readily see the difference.

Until well into the nineteenth century, two row was the typical brewing barley (although one historian told me that in the pioneer areas of North America, brewers probably weren't picky, using whatever they could get). It was hardier than six row but not as productive. Gradually, as the brewing industry became more industrialized, six-row barley muscled out its less productive relative and has been used pretty much exclusively for most of the last century to brew beer in North America. Another advantage of six row is that it works particularly well in brewing in conjunction with other grains, such as corn or rice, that are cheaper than barley. Beers made with these adjuncts, which is what they are called, revolutionized brewing in North America, giving us many of the dominant beers of the late twentieth century—Budweiser and Labatt Blue, for example. The adjuncts made them—depending on your point of view—either smooth and crisp, or bland and uninteresting.

But two-row barley hadn't been counted out just yet. With the interest in craft brewing that started in the 1980s and has accelerated over the past decade, niche and home beer makers have rediscovered this older grain. Coming full circle, malt made from two row is the preferred choice of most craft brewers today.

This history I knew fairly well. But that was all I knew. Of the actual business of finding and growing two-row barley, I was blissfully ignorant. Not that I was worried: my father once said that the best business to get into was running a hardware store. You bought the store and then your customers taught you what you needed to know. That was pretty much my plan where barley growing was concerned—my ignorance would be my most useful tool. Many people out there like to teach. I planned to give them plenty of opportunities. I started calling seed and feed places, a process I later came to think of as phone farming.

The first thing I learned was that not all two-row barley was malting barley, which was the type I needed. Uh-oh. I wasn't quite sure what the other kind of two-row barley was used for (people didn't say exactly), but it wasn't for malting. I also learned that telling a seed company you wanted two-row barley was about as helpful as walking into a car dealership and announcing that you wanted to buy an American sedan. There was a myriad of varieties. Metcalfe and Kendall, Harrington and Manley. Some grew taller than others, some nurtured faster, some were more resistant to fusarium—whatever that was.

Alas, the second thing I learned was that by waiting until early May 2011, I was starting too late. The bulk of North America's malting barley is grown out west—North Dakota in the United States, Saskatchewan and Alberta in Canada. For a variety of reasons I would learn more about later, very little is grown in the east. In my part of Ontario, the feed suppliers don't get much call for malting barley. What they do get, they typically have in by February. I should, they told me, have ordered earlier.

I'd thought that, for convenience's sake, I'd order it from a supplier near our farm in the valley—best not to have to lug it too far. I started with Renfrew—with a population of just over eight thousand, our closest "big town." No go. Then Pakenham, the next "big" place after Renfrew, home to a five-span stone bridge and about two thousand souls. Same story. After that, farther afield. Perth, about an hour's drive away. Again, the same story: forget it. I left messages with feedstores across eastern and southern Ontario. Kingston, Belleville, Picton—I phoned myself halfway west along Lake Ontario with no results.

No barley, no beer. As I looked up phone numbers on the Internet, I could hear Catharine's voice: *I told you to order* (no); *you always put everything off* (not true); *that means no perfect keg for you* (true, alas). I contemplated wading into the St. Lawrence.

Then it hit me: forget stores, try the suppliers. In the course of my research, I came across a type of two-row malting barley called CDC Stratus. The seed company that sold CDC Stratus had a 519 area code—that put it somewhere in southwestern Ontario. I could leave in the morning, pick up the seed and then come back the same day. An eight-hour round-trip, max. I was desperate. I called them.

Only to find out that I had it all wrong. I didn't want CDC Stratus, the receptionist told me. I want Newdale. That was the standard two-row malting barley. She gave me their sales rep's phone number. She might—just might—be able to help me. When I hung up, I called the rep on Skype. As I dialed, a call was coming through on my landline. It was someone called Lindsay, calling from the feedstore in Picton. She had become interested in my request and had been asking around there. What I needed, she confirmed, was Newdale. She had a bag. Did I want it?

From absolute ignorance to success in forty-five minutes. I was off to a good start.

"YOU LOOK LIKE BARLEY PEOPLE"

"YOU LOOK LIKE barley people."

I was intrigued by Lindsay's comment. She seemed like a sensible young woman, plainly dressed and straightforward in manner, and she delivered her message in a straightforward way. She didn't expand on it, and I didn't ask her to—I think I understood what she meant.

We were at a feedstore on the outskirts of Picton, an incredibly scenic town in Ontario's Prince Edward County. "The county," as it's universally called, occupies a blocky peninsula almost entirely surrounded by Lake Ontario, scalloped by sandy bays bitten off by the lake on its western edges and slashed through its middle by the huge inverted Z that is the Bay of Quinte. Located at the end of a long reach of the bay, Picton boasts some of the greatest freshwater sailing in the world. But right now, on a hot, humid day in early May, more like July than a central Canadian spring, our minds were focused on land, not sea.

For the past decade or so, the county—not much more than two hours' drive from Toronto—has been experiencing what can best be termed "rural gentrification." It's not just that bed and breakfasts have set up in old farmhouses and that tired general stores have given way to art galleries and scratch-made ice cream parlors. The very crops in the ground have changed to reflect an affluent urban sensibility of the sort exhibited by people who want the artisanal or the local and are willing to pay through the nose. Vineyards, in other words, have been taking the place of tomato farms.

The feedstore straddled these two worlds. The parking lot was a mix of Ford F-150s and Range Rovers. In the main store, horse-related tack, a sure sign of rural upward mobility, seemed to be edging out more traditional feed shovels and electric fence kits. The annex where they kept seed and feed, on the far side of the parking lot, was planted firmly in the past, however—right down to a trio of elderly male locals seated on a bench inside the door indulging in that old rural tradition of hanging out at the feedstore. Our request for Newdale two-row barley identified us, however tenuously, as part of the newer world. Barley people.

This was ironic. The county had once been at the center of the North American barley trade, sending schooners laden with the stuff across Lake Ontario to Oswego, New York, from where it headed by barge through the state's canal system to the Hudson, bound ultimately for New York City. In the 1880s, you could make a lot of money growing barley. The proceeds from just one year in the business were enough to buy you one of the large brick farmhouses that still dot the county. Then in the early 1890s, the American government introduced the so-called McKinley Tariff, designed to protect American manufacturing and agriculture, and the industry—and the county—collapsed.

Again ironically, the county was never really suited for producing barley—it's too hot in the summer and, thanks to being nearly surrounded by water, too wet. These conditions are ideal for the growth of ergot, a mold that is the distant, naturally occurring cousin of LSD. Ergot was blamed for outbreaks of St. Vitus' dance in the Middle Ages. This was when the peasants would go crazy from eating bread made with ergot-infested barley and begin dancing manically, fornicating publicly and so on. Sounds like fun, actually. Indeed, it may explain why the county's barley was so popular back in the day. I once had a chat just outside a venerable local pub with a sales rep for a county-based craft brewery who tried to tell me, smiling but completely sincere, that ergot was the precise reason why people liked beer made with Prince Edward County barley—it was like drinking liquid LSD. Today's world, however, takes a rather more jaundiced view of psychotropic additives. A few years ago, some boutique growers in Prince Edward tried to revive the county's barley industry—only to have their crop rejected because of ergot.

Musing on the possibility of creating my own beer with a special buzz, I handed over the $18.95 for my fifty-pound bag of Newdale. So taken with Millie was the man who fetched it for us that he insisted on carrying it for us across the parking to our waiting Honda Fit. I didn't complain. Fifty pounds isn't all that much weight, but the bulk of the bag surprised me. Made of some sort of tightly woven plastic material, it was much bigger than a bag of cement but loose and floppy. I'd never given much thought before to what fifty pounds of barley seed would look like. It took up most of the hatch of our Fit. A big jump from those little packets of carrot seeds you buy at the supermarket.

I MAY NOT have known anything about farming, but I had the one indispensable accessory that any would-be agrarian needs: a farm. Two hundred acres or so in the Ottawa Valley. My wife and a group of people she has known since university bought it in the mid-1970s. They'd realized the dream that a lot of people had in the tail end of the back-to-the-land era. When they talk about the acreage, it is invariably referred to as "the farm." When I describe it to people, they often say, "Oh, it's just like *The Big Chill*." And I tell them, "Yes, but only if *The Big Chill* had been written by Harold Pinter." Sometimes I think it's what life would have been like in one of those minor European courts in the eighteenth century—generally pleasant and undemanding but requiring one to keep an eye on shifting alliances and intrigues. Seemingly trivial facts and events—which way the door should open on the new refrigerator, for example—can be freighted with subtext and the ghosts of grievances past. Factions quickly emerge and heated arguments erupt. The surroundings, however, make these odd blow-ups easy to stomach—over the years, the farm has morphed from an Insulbrick-covered box with a sagging enclosed porch into a gray clapboard palace—nine bedrooms, a glass-doored fireplace in the living room, an Italian-tiled sunroom and a long veranda that wouldn't look out of place on a Sri Lankan tea plantation. And like a plantation, others do all the work. Harold, the tenant farmer, keeps cattle on the land and cuts the hay. Two bearded beekeeping brothers—fundamentalist francophones, in fact, just to keep the alliteration rolling—keep a collection of hives at the bottom of one field. (I often wonder how the nudist colony located on the next farm over feels about that.)

"YOU LOOK LIKE BARLEY PEOPLE"

Writing these last sentences, I am aware of just how odd they sound. You need to understand them in their proper context. You need to understand the Ottawa Valley.

How to describe the valley? Well, it is a valley, yes, the watershed of the Ottawa River. Near the river it looks pretty much as you might expect—a flat alluvial plain. Move inland from that, and the landscape changes dramatically—to steep, rocky, heavily forested hills, the valleys between them marked by lakes and fast-running rivers flecked with rapids. There are farms tucked here and there, usually in the rare pockets of soil between the hills. Many of them still boast rail fences and their original log houses. A few have been in the same family since the land was cleared in the 1860s. The height of land to the west, where Algonquin Park lies, empties most of the clouds formed over the Great Lakes. As a result, the valley is one of the driest farming areas in Ontario. This would, in theory, make it good for growing barley. So would the long, cold winters that linger on into what other regions call spring. This year, on a weekend in early May, looking from the highest spot at our farm, we could see snow on the top of the long stretch of high hills a few miles away known as the Madawaska Highlands. The upside was that snowmelt had been locked into the ground, offsetting what was likely to be summer drought, and the cold had killed off molds and pests a warmer climate might harbor. Again, that was the theory.

Standing there looking over the hills, the fields just starting to show the pale yellow-green of spring, I thought about how the valley's geography—isolating, yes, but with fast-running rivers that allowed lumbering to flourish over the centuries—had shaped a unique way of life. It's entirely appropriate that our highlands are the northernmost limit of a long chain of old mountains that run down through the eastern United States, culminating in the Appalachians, a thousand miles south of our farm. Valley folks and hill people have a lot in common. A strong dose of Scots-Irish blood, mingled in the valley with French-Canadian and Polish. Economies based on seasonal work and small-scale farming. Deep distrust of revenuers and other forms of officialdom (signs proclaiming "Government back off—This land is ours" dot the region). Distinctive ways of speaking. Their own dances and music—as one smart aleck put it, people in the valley don't eat with spoons; they play them. But they also play the fiddle and the accordion, weaving jigs and reels and pumping out polkas. Hillbillies and valley people share some of the same hobbies, too—bootlegging, dynamite fishing and jacklighting, a highly illegal form of nighttime deer hunting using a headlight and a car battery.

They're not entirely the same people, of course. I get the feeling that life in Appalachia is grim; that people there are just scraping along. By contrast, life in the valley seems joyfully, effortlessly absurd. A sign in the local supermarket announces, completely deadpan, "Ice—Regular or Diet." The anecdote that for me best sums up the valley came from a doctor friend of ours. One night she was working the emergency room at Renfrew when an ambulance brought in a local farmer. He'd been run over by a pickup truck. His own, he claimed. His dog had been at the wheel.

So if I sometimes felt a little self-conscious about my brewing project, about just how ignorant I was about what I was trying to do, I didn't have to worry. No one in a place like this was going to pay much attention to some smart-ass city fellow sowing and reaping a crop by hand.

If, that is, I got the chance. Spring had arrived very late this year. The ground was still very wet, which meant farmers couldn't get out to the fields on their tractors. A few weeks before, I'd spoken vaguely to Harold about plowing an area for me to plant barley in, but at that point, I hadn't even figured out where exactly I wanted my crop to go. Last week I found out that he was going into the hospital on May 10 for a hip replacement. He would be out of commission for weeks.

A cheerful, ruddy-faced man in his sixties, Harold is part of the local gentry in this part of the valley. He and various members of his extended clan own or rent farms all around our area. For many years, he drove the township snowplow (a hereditary sinecure that has since been passed on to his brother); now in his "retirement," he works the farm. Only once have I seen Harold without a flannel shirt and a baseball cap, even in the height of summer. On that occasion, I had dropped by his house, notable for the three pickup trucks parked outside, and he had answered the door garbed in what I thought of as his leisure wear—pilled polyester sweatpants and a T-shirt bearing the words "Las Vegas: Sin City since 1905." Harold boasts one of the purest—and least penetrable—Ottawa Valley accents I have ever heard: "Da' rain was comin' down ticker dan da hair on a hound's back." He always seems to be smiling, too—I suspect that he finds the farm members' requests ("Could you move your cows? There are flies" or "Do you have to spread manure on the fields?") to be a source of amusement. His eyes certainly twinkled the first time I told him about my barley scheme.

I'd been phoning Harold for about a week to see if he'd be able to plow my field, but I hadn't been able to reach him. I'd hoped that he would drop by the farm sometime during the weekend, but he hadn't. That meant I was going to have to seek him out. I don't know why, but I felt odd about doing this. Part of me worried that it was somehow patronizing, like I was the dowager duchess descending on a humble tenant's cottage. *Downton Abbey* played out among the pines and the rock piles. Another part of me was aware of how tenuous my position was. Harold doesn't have a deal with me; I am strictly the "spouse of." We'd never talked money—how much or indeed any.

ONE OF MY biggest challenges had been to figure out exactly how big an area I needed to plant. Mentally I said to myself that what I needed was "Oh, about an acre." I didn't really know how large that was. But the thing about nature is you always seem to need a hell of a lot of something—two tons of krill to feed a whale for a day, for example. Assuming all nature followed similar laws, an acre would be good for a couple of barrels of beer.

I felt real delight when I learned from the barley page on the University of North Dakota's website that one acre in that state produced enough barley to make 28,800 bottles of beer. Even if one of those bottles should happen to fall, that was still a hell of a lot of beer on the wall. I did some calculating. If I drank two a day, I would be drinking the same beer for the next thirty-seven years. Even if I had a friend visit, it would take me close to two decades to get rid of it all. I'd probably be pretty tired of it by then.

Instead, I decided that I needed a far more modest strip, about thirty feet by one hundred. Three thousand square feet, 7 percent of an acre or thereabouts. I understood that I wouldn't get the yields of a real farmer in North Dakota (which would have worked out to more than two thousand bottles), but this would still, I reckoned, give me enough barley to make several brews. On balance it would have been nice to have more barley than I could possible use, but if I planned to fertilize, weed and harvest my patch by hand—and I had no equipment so that was pretty much understood—it was smartest to go with the smallest patch of barley possible. I'd spent some time talking to Peter Johnson, the barley expert with the Ontario Ministry of Agriculture and Food. Peter told me that there wasn't much malting barley grown in Ontario, though some farmers do plant it in cooler and drier parts of the province. Planting is a bit of a balancing act—barley doesn't, as he put it, "like to get its feet wet." But you also don't want it to be too dry.

The area I picked out fit these categories, generally. It was a sloping bit of hill, just inside our gate, with a southern exposure and good drainage. I'd also had a chance to look at a soil map for Renfrew County, a wild swirling mass of color that looked like a cross between a Rorschach test and a Jackson Pollock painting. This tiny little patch was sandier than anywhere else on the farm, which made it our best potential barley patch. Water can trickle down to the roots in sandy soils; clay soils tend to hold it. I'd marked out the area with small metal stakes and pieces of fluorescent tape so that even if I were not around, Harold would know where I wanted him to plow.

When I got home on the night of May 8, I had a call from Harold on my voice mail: "I've dug your garden for you."

BARLEY GENERALLY TAKES about ninety days to mature. In most parts of the province, they tell you not to plant much later than mid-May. In cooler areas, and I think that includes mine, you can push it to the end of May. But no later, Peter told me. After that, you can't get crop insurance (not that I could have anyway, but I took it as a marker of risk)—as far as the insurers are concerned, the danger of failure is already too high.

Time was getting tight. We'd had a wet spring—too wet. We'd been lucky that Harold had been able to plow my little hillside at all before he checked into hospital. The flat bottom land was still so sodden that if he had tried to disk it, his tractor would have sunk in. Now we were into late May. If we didn't get the barley in soon, we might find ourselves in trouble at the opposite end of the growing season, hit with a frost before we'd had time to harvest.

Before we could even think about planting, I had to make sure the ground was ready. Peter from the Ministry of Agriculture had given me an easy test. Dig out a lump of dirt the size of a golf ball from your field. Take it from about three inches down, he told me. Hold it in your hand and jam your thumb into it. If it breaks into big chunks, the soil isn't ready. If it crumbles, it is. Don't even think about trying to plant if it's just mud. I dug out a lump and pushed my thumb into it; the ball crumbled into nice flakes. It was the crack of nine thirty on Saturday, May 21, and I had a full day ahead of me.

Barley needs nitrogen. From my research, I knew that the usual amount worked out to about fifty pounds an acre. Nicely seasoned manure is about 2 percent nitrogen. So for my plot, I estimated I would have to dump about three hundred pounds of manure before I could start seeding.

You could think of fertilizing, at least the way I did it, as a programming loop: take one late-model Honda Fit. Put down back seat, cover with plastic, add a shovel and two large plastic tubs. Back car down the narrow lane between a collapsing log piggery and the sagging gray plank outbuilding where Harold stashes his manure. (Well, his cows' manure, actually.) Drag tubs and shovel inside. Find oldest, driest manure, take shovel and load into plastic tub until about half-full. Lift into previously positioned wheelbarrow then wheel to waiting Honda Fit. Fill and load second tub. Drive Fit two-thirds of the way up the hill, stop. Set hand brake and get out. Remove tubs. Lift tub into second previously positioned wheelbarrow. Push off driveway into tall grass. Curse wheelbarrow's flat tire. Struggle across rough ground, turn right into future field of barley, tip barrow and dump manure. Repeat. And repeat. And repeat.

In all, I made ten trips up the hill. I'd planned six, but three hundred pounds of manure didn't seem to go very far. In the end, I had loaded and dumped more than five hundred pounds. Catharine helped me rake in the first two loads, but for most of the day I was on my own. Raking in wasn't particularly difficult—you're just dragging the rake through the top couple of inches of dirt, making sure the manure gets broken up and nicely mixed in. Shoveling and lifting and struggling with the wheelbarrow were all harder. But raking in was the most time-consuming. I remember walking down to the farmhouse for water when I was about halfway done, and the clock said two thirty. I finished fertilizing just before six.

I had given a lot of thought to seeding. But, admittedly, this was mostly from a presentation point of view. At first, I had envisioned myself with a bag over one shoulder, tossing seed casually with one hand as I strode across the field—a bit like the logo of Simon and Schuster, I think, or some sort of folkloric figure—Johnny Barleyseed, say. And I thought I could give it a sort of ironic take by using my old newspaper delivery bag. But one of the other farm members came up with what proved to be a much better idea—one of those little contraptions that people use to seed their lawns. You know them—a little red hopper with two wheels and a long handle, and a switch to control the rate of distribution. You set it, load it, and then you push it merrily along the ground, scattering seed before you, all thanks to a mini mechanical Onan. The mainstay of every suburban dad.

Of course, these seeders are designed for relatively small, relatively smooth lawns, not farmers' fields. As I pushed it along, the hopper bucked and jumped, bumping up-down-down-right-left-even—*hunh!*—stopped dead by a large rock or clod of dirt, jamming the handle into my stomach. Maybe, I thought, sowing by hand was the way to go. I picked up the seeder, tucked it under my arm and began scooping out handfuls of barley and scattering them around, a technique that left large areas of my plot bald and others heaped with seed. Even worse. So back I went to the thump, jump, bump of pushing the seeder through the field. The interesting thing was, it worked. I had determined how much seed I was going to need to cover my patch, and the machine ran out precisely at the end.

This spring had been great for blackflies, and I had a cloud of them around my head as I toiled—happily, I swallowed a mere three. But they worked on me around my sock line, where my arms stuck out of my shirt and, worst of all, along my hat line—someone later remarked that I looked like a man who had been wearing a crown of thorns. I felt like one, too. They got worse as the day went along, and by the time I had finished seeding, they were at their height. Now I had to rake in the barley seed, which meant going over my field once more.

I'd started the day wearing my smart straw fedora, but because I had been sweating so profusely, by noon it had the look and some of the consistency of wet shredded wheat. I had switched to a baseball cap in the afternoon, and as I bent over to rake, I could see sweat dripping off the bill. I learned later that, below me, as I worked, the others had sat in the farmhouse's sunroom discussing whether I would make it or not. Not "make it," I fear, in the sense of finish the job, but in the sense of survive. I suspect that, to interested observers of my day's activities, the idea of me facedown in a field and quite, quite dead, seemed all too plausible.

It was not to be. I finished up that evening at eight. Exhausted, dehydrated and covered in bloody bites. I had been at it for ten hours, more or less.

I SPENT A fair bit of time lying in bed the next morning, trying to decide whether I could walk. What didn't hurt, itched. I could walk, as it turned out, which was good, because Sunday was hop planting day. Apart from the area where I had planted my barley, the farm's soil is made up of a lot of clay (not counting the considerable stretches of rock, that is), and clay isn't ideal for hops. They like it a bit sandier. Fortunately, the township was doing some work on the road, so we were able to borrow sand from the big pile they had dumped nearby. We mixed this with rotted manure, and then I created three small beds, one for each variety of hop, with three plants in each bed, the beds dotted along the south side of the henhouse. (That's what Harold, who built it when he lived here as a boy, long before the city folk bought the farm, calls it. The farm members now refer to it as the "coopio," having turned it into an artists' studio of sorts.) Working on an extension ladder, I screwed eye hooks into the fascia of the henhouse and we ran long lines of jute twine down and anchored them in the soil for the hops to climb. That Sunday, May 22, was not a good day to plant—too clear and sunny. Transplant anything in those conditions and it's going to wilt. We'd have to head home after planting, so if the weather stayed that way, the hops might just expire before we got back. But we had no choice. The plants had to go in—otherwise, they might not set cones before the first frost. Happily, as we left the farm a few hours later, it started to rain.

Even with the rain, though, I realized that this first week would be key for getting the hops to settle in and the barley to sprout. If things hadn't worked out by the time we returned, I could probably save the hops—the garden hose would easily reach. But given the size of my field and its location up the hill from the house, there would be much less I could do about the barley.

This was something I was beginning to understand about rural life: the lack of control. If you're a farmer, you're at the mercy of the elements. You may need to plant by such and such a date; if it doesn't stop raining, too bad. And if it doesn't start raining? That's too bad, too. In other jobs, you can work around these problems: decide to work on the weekend instead of the week, reschedule tasks, pay extra for express delivery, whatever. Farming doesn't allow for that.

One good thing I had found out from my reading about barley: it was a very simple crop to grow. You don't need to water it, the books and websites told me, and you don't have to worry about weeds. A simple crop for a simple man. It seemed a good fit.

Two

HIT BY A WORT BOMB

ONCE I HAD finished planting and was back home in Kingston, I felt that I could switch my focus a little, leave farming behind and concentrate on honing my brewing chops. One of the things I had decided really early on in the project—in keeping with my whole making-my-ignorance-work-for-me approach—was to spend some time working with really serious brewers.

As a start, I had spent a morning in late April with Peter Snell at the Kingston Brewing Company. The oldest still-running pub in Ontario to brew its own beer (and the second to be licensed), the brewpub, as it is commonly called, is located in a red brick Victorian hulk that once housed the city's telegraph office. The 1949 International Harvester red delivery truck parked outside makes it easy to spot. The pub is definitely worth a visit, if only to take in its incredible collection of "breweriana." Pump handles, bar mats, give-away trays, bottle openers—almost anything that can carry a logo and a brand name—from breweries worldwide, both thriving and defunct, fill display cases, festoon the staircase and run up walls decorated with stenciled barley heads. Peter's workplace, the brewery part of the brewpub, is a white-tiled room dominated by chest-high stainless steel vats and visible through the sliding glass doors behind the small bar. The brewery offers tours—a fact I find incredible, as the day I spent watching him at work we were constantly in each other's way. You'd have to smear a party of six with butter to squeeze them all in. I've seen larger walk-in closets. It was an interesting way to spend a morning, but I didn't learn all that much. Peter brews using malt extract. This practice was fairly standard for brewpubs back when the Kingston Brewing Company opened in the 1980s, but this sort of brewing has moved on a long way since then. Unfortunately, the brewpub's equipment—and the cramped spaces that Peter has to work with—limits what he can do.

I CERTAINLY HAD a lot to learn about the *how* of brewing; I had already started thinking about the *what*. Assuming the barley came up and my hops flourished, what would I make from them? Yes, to be sure, I was brewing beer. But honestly? That isn't all that different from some mad scientist saying he wants to create "life." Okay, what kind of life? A blue whale or a head of lettuce? No matter how much it might seem like it when drinking more mainstream products, there is no generic beer, any more than there is generic life.

Right off I knew my beer would not be organic. It's too bad that organic is such a binary thing—either you are or you aren't—because I figured it could squeak in as "mostly" organic or "largely" organic. But my barley seed had been treated with a chemical fungicide, so I was out before I even got going. But organic is a mixed blessing. Not long after I planted, the *Globe and Mail* had an interesting piece about Mill Street Organic Lager. Founded in 2002, Mill Street is a cutting-edge craft brewery in Toronto that consistently wins awards for its beers. To create their organic lager and make it truly organic meant not just using organically grown ingredients but storing the malt in a dedicated hopper at the brewery and having the barley malted at a dedicated organic maltster. This requirement has some odd consequences. The only organic maltster in North America is in Washington State. The organic hops came all the way from New Zealand. My suspicion is that although the finished beer is in fact organic, its carbon footprint is horrendous—probably worse than sitting in an idling old Cadillac drinking a Coors Light.

One idea I did have was to try something historic. For a few reasons. One, I like old-fashioned beers. Two, I thought old-fashioned would be in some ways easier. Older beers were brewed using basic ingredients and simple equipment—a big open kitchen pot would do you just fine, along with a glass carboy to store the beer in. Precisely the kind of kit I had.

So what then? I got one potentially exciting idea from a fellow Kingstonian, Alan McLeod. Alan is a lawyer who works for the City of Kingston. An expansive man and an all-round food and drink enthusiast, he possesses one of the finest Boris Johnson hairdos on this side of the Atlantic. His witty and informative A Good Beer blog was one of the first beer blogs anywhere, and at one point was garnering more daily visitors than the Guinness website. (Alan is also a vintage baseball enthusiast. He and a group of like-minded individuals get together several times a summer to play baseball using the equipment and rules of the mid-nineteenth century. Eight balls and you walk.) From his website, I learned that Alan was involved in another historic endeavor: the Albany Ale Project. He had been researching and posting on Albany ale for years, and when I first read about it, I was very interested. I had been meaning to give him a copy of my last book, so when we met at our local brewpub, I got him to tell me more about this mythic beer.

As far back as the eighteenth century, Albany, New York, had been America's first brewing capital, what Milwaukee or St. Louis would later become. Local brewers (including one Joshua Vassar, as in Vassar College) shipped beer throughout the thirteen colonies and even across the Atlantic to England. Plenty of people who first settled Kingston were Loyalists fleeing north from the Albany area. It was very possible that they not only knew Albany ale, but also continued to drink it once they arrived here, and perhaps even to make it.

The idea of a specific local beer made with local ingredients and in roughly our part of the world (Albany's a three-hour drive from us) seemed too good to be true. It was. As I learned from following Alan's blog and talking to him, and later from joining the Albany ale Facebook page, absolutely no one seemed to know what was in Albany ale. There were old ads and yellowed newspaper reports, ledger entries and bills of sale. A few years after this, Alan and his fellow enthusiasts managed find an actual recipe, but at this point no one had any idea what it was. At best, they had clues—it used hard well water pumped from far underground and may have been made with a single malt. I suppose I could have brewed anything and claimed it was Albany ale, but that didn't seem right somehow.

To get more ideas, I e-mailed the noted Canadian beer historian Ian Bowering, telling him what I was up to. Ian replied that if I wanted to be really historic, I should forget malted barley and go with honey, maple syrup or spruce needles. Happily, he also sent me a list of the top beers in eastern Ontario at the time of Confederation in 1867, in order of popularity:

Dark ale
Porter
Pale ale
Amber pale ale
India pale ale
Cream ale
Double stout

Barley wine
Champagne ale
Mild beer
Scotch ale
Stout

It seemed lengthy, but going through the list actually made life easier. All the pale ales, I assumed, were probably offerings from nascent industrial brewers (industrial, in this case, being relative), because pale ales only became possible with indirect kilning of malt—not a step a farmhouse brewer in a remote corner of the valley could take back then. So I could put them aside. Ditto the cream ale, porter and stout. I didn't know what to make of the mention of champagne ale. From what little I have gleaned, it seems to have been a beer fermented with champagne yeast and sometimes even stored like champagne, in bottles laid on their sides and carefully given quarter turns while fermenting. Could a part of the world where hogs still rooted in streets lined with board sidewalks have really made ale using champagne yeast? It seemed hard to credit.

That left me with three possible ales: dark, Scotch and mild. I thought I might try mild. It's a venerable brew and, as its name suggests, low in alcohol—generally 4 percent by volume. So not too strong (beers today are typically about 5 percent alcohol by volume). As the name mild might also suggest, it's not too hoppy. All in, it seemed the sort of ale that a humble artisan might have drunk at lunch way back when.

So by late May, I had my *what*, at least potentially, and I was starting to learn more about the *how*. My crops were doing their thing. It was just a case of keeping my head down and moving forward.

SCARCELY FOUR DAYS passed after planting before I could get back to the farm, but I fretted while I was away. If I'm honest, however, I have to admit that my presence wouldn't have made much difference. Either it rained or it didn't. The next time we rolled down the driveway was on May 26—just in time for the perfect rain. It wasn't hard; it just kept going and going and going. Never had I been so happy to be housebound.

All nine hop plants had taken, and most of them were sending out tendrils. I had been more worried about my barley. When we had left the previous Sunday afternoon, it had been spitting rain fitfully, and I don't think all that much fell in the end. Or in the days after that. The ground in my barley field was looking pretty dry when we rolled past it. (I also noticed some seeds just lying on the ground along the edge of the road, which dismayed me. I don't know if it did any good, but I buried them.) This was a good soaking rain, precisely what the barley needed. It rained during the night and kept going the next morning—perfect for germination. By the time we left the farm late Sunday, the barley was starting to come up, a tracery of the palest green, denser in some places than others, over the lumpy black soil. We'd been lucky. I read that weekend that only about 1 percent of Ontario's cereal crop had even been planted by the end of May, forget having germinated. It had been too wet. The heavy equipment that commercial farmers use would have simply sunk into the mud. Harold mentioned he had a hell of a time disking our vegetable garden. Sometimes, a man with a wheelbarrow and a lawn seeder can get ahead of the big boys.

BEFORE I'D PLANTED, I started my second batch of beer. If you wanted to compare beer making to playing the harmonica, that first batch had been me wheezing my way through "Row, row, row your boat." Now I had to step it up a little—to the level of Alanis Morissette or Bob Dylan, say.

My first beer had been a total kit concoction—wort (the name for the sticky fluid you get from adding malt to water) and an envelope of yeast. The next step up was to brew using malt extract. Now sometimes going this route isn't much more complex than what we had done for our first brew. You get a big can of malt extract with the hops already added, a packet of yeast and maybe a small container filled with pellet hops (concentrated hops compressed into something resembling rabbit food) if the extract hasn't been hopped already. You pour the extract into boiling water, stir it in, let it bubble a bit and then cool it before tossing in what are referred to as carbonation drops. I suspect these are the yeast combined with some sort of food. To be honest, you can make some halfway decent beer this way. You can play around with these kits a little, too.

Or you can try for something a little more complex and, flavor-wise, a little more interesting. Most home brew places sell something called pale malt extract, which is made from two-row barley and could be called a basic building block of craft beer. It's sold as an intensely sticky and viscous syrup or as a dried powder that's produced by extracting the sugars from malted barley. Either way, once you add it to water and heat it up, you get your basic wort or brewing fluid. What makes it a building block isn't just its flavor: pale two-row malt also provides the yeast with an optimal diet, allowing it to produce alcohol and carbon dioxide very efficiently from the barley's sugars. Starting with it, you can add different malts, grains, even fruit or vegetables, hops and the yeast of your choice and make pretty much any style of beer in the world.

Some people look down their noses at brewing with extract, and I think it's fair to say that the home brewer's dream is to make beer using only grain—that is, malted barley and other grains in their natural state—but plenty of really good home brews can be created from a base of malt extract. Still, I've heard one knowledgeable home brewer claim that beers made with extract always have a slightly caramelized flavor, from cooking down the malt solution. I am not so sure.

Get into making beer and one thing you quickly discover, in the words of the James Brown song "It's a Man's Man's Man's World." Go back to the preindustrial era, and brewing beer was women's work. Not now. There are women who brew, but not that many. I mention this only because of one thing: equipment. I suspect that if women made all the beer, they'd get by with whatever pots and pans they already had lying around in the kitchen. Not men. Men need gear. Visit a great home brewing store, shop online or check out the ads in *Brew Your Own* magazine (a valuable resource, by the way) and the selection is astounding: false-bottomed mash tuns and nitrogen kegging systems. Erlenmeyer flasks and refractometers (to this day, I have no idea what the hell either of these objects is or does). *Two hundred and forty liter* home fermentation tanks—just the ticket if you don't have a wife or a job. One firm offers a bare-bones, two-propane burner home brewing system featuring stainless steel kegs and braided hose lines for a modest $1,999.95. The Iranians use a similar system to enrich uranium.

But all of that kit paled when I met Grayson, Dave and Randy. Technologically savvy amateur beer makers—at least one has a degree in electrical engineering—they had set up their brewing outfit in a disused creamery in the Northumberland Hills north of Lake Ontario. Charlie Papazian, the dean of home brewers, had described it as the most sophisticated amateur setup in North America. Entering it was like stepping into an ICU run by a Bond villain. Things that beeped, guys hovering over valves and dials, muttered consultations, an atmosphere of tense concentration dominated by a stainless steel mash tun (a "tun" being a fancy brewing word for big tank). When they were boiling the wort, they could hold it to within a quarter of a degree in temperature. Grayson, Dave and Randy brew in 350-liter lots. That's something like three hundred bottles each. They will never run out and they will never need to buy beer again. Watching them brew was an awe-inspiring sight. But looking at all the gleaming modern equipment, I wondered how beer ever got made in the old days.

Probably in something closer to my more modest setup, I suspect. I planned to brew using the bare minimum: a large white plastic tub capable of holding twenty liters or about five gallons. A glass carboy of similar capacity. A rubber bung with an air lock. A long, hard, clear plastic tube with a bend in it called a racking cane, a section of clear plastic hose to stick on it and an end piece with a gravity lock—all needed for moving the brew from one container to another with minimal mess.

My hydrometer, for measuring specific gravity, would be an invaluable aid. Water's specific gravity is 1.0000, and anything higher indicates that something is dissolved in the water. In the case of wort, specific gravity gives you a measure of how much sugar is dissolved in the starting brew, which is a guide to how strong the finished beer will be. The gravity will drop as the yeast turns the sugars into alcohol, which has a lower specific gravity than water, and carbon dioxide, which bubbles away. A beer might start with a gravity of 1.055 and end with one of, say, 1.012. (It will never end up at or below 1.000, because of lingering sugars and other dissolved stuff.) The last two digits give you a rough measure of the beer's final strength—so the starting reading of 1.055 would translate to an alcohol content of 5.5 percent. The specific gravity also tells you when the beer has finished fermenting. When you get uniform readings day after day, it's time to bottle.

I also had a thermometer—very important for brewing properly, especially when using whole grain. Speaking of which, I bought myself a grain mill, which resembled a meat grinder with a round plate stuck over the end where the hamburger would normally come out. Turns out, the company that made it also made my tortilla press. Talk about exploiting niche markets. I agonized about a five-gallon pot. I checked out a heavyweight beauty at a nearby kitchenware store but was put off by the price—seventy bucks. I went out and got one at Canadian Tire, one of those blue enamel jobs people use for making jam, which cost less than half that. A bit of a false economy, I later discovered.

Once I had my pot, though, I could start work on one essential piece of brewing gear that I wanted to make myself. A wort chiller.

If I were asked to explain what a wort chiller does, I'd say it deals with a paradox and an enemy. Here's the paradox. When you brew, you bring your wort to the boil and keep it there for a long time, generally an hour. The next stage in the brewing process is pitching (adding) the yeast. Except high temperatures kill yeast. So you want the wort much cooler—around sixty-eight degrees Fahrenheit. You could of course just wait, but here's where the enemy comes in. Bacteria could get into the beer and spoil it. The longer it sits, the more likely this is. (People weren't aware of this in the old days, of course. One of the venerable brewing texts I consulted actually recommended leaving beer to cool in open vats—outdoors.) The wort gets cloudy, too, from sitting around. So you want hot wort cooled quickly.

Enter the wort chiller. I made mine from twenty-plus feet of coiled copper tubing by clamping plastic hoses on each end. When I finished boiling my wort, I'd take it off the heat, drop the coil—after sterilizing it—into my pot, hook it to the faucet and run cold water through it. This would drop the temperature quickly. The hose attached to the tap by means of a neat adapter I had rigged out of plumbing pieces. One fitting screwed onto the tap once I removed the aerator. Another fitting connected to this so that it could fit into a third, broader fitting, which in turn hooked to a fitting that then tapered down and was jammed into the tubing. (*The knee bone's connected to the…*)

All was ready. I immediately began sweeping floors, wiping counters, emptying trash cans. That done, I got in the car and went to Toronto for a few days. My signature work habits (shirk habits, really), honed over decades of employment, were proving readily adaptable to the business of brewing.

I was anxious because this was a big step for me. Our first effort, the kit, had been almost foolproof (though we did our best). But I really could blow this one and end up with nothing to show for it. I was also a little nervous because I wasn't sure exactly *what* I was making. I'd found three good mild ale recipes—one for a dark mild, one for a ruby and one for a gold. But because Kingston is a relatively small city with a relatively small number of home brewers, my local home brew place didn't have all of the ingredients I needed for any one of them. So in the same way as I had been using my ignorance as a tool, I decided to make a virtue of necessity. Among my (few) other gifts is a facility at baking pies. In fact, I am sometimes referred to as the pie man. (By me, mostly. Others call me that, too, but you can almost see the little quote marks around it when they say it.) Anyway, one thing you learn about baking pies—peach, apple, cherry—they are generally the same. Sure, each one has its own little differences, but put in the right amount of fruit and the right amount of sugar, make a decent crust and bake it at the proper temperature and you won't go far wrong. I was gambling that brewing is sort of like baking—it's all about manipulating grain. What I was attempting would incorporate the do-able, if not the best, elements of all three recipes. But if I kept to the broad strokes, I'd be all right.

When it came time to brew, what I did was essentially the same as I would do for all my future brews.

First, I poured three gallons of well water into my pot. I used well water from the farm—chlorinated water can give beer harsh flavors, and our local tap water has a vaguely algae taste to it. While the water was heating on the cook top in our narrow little Kingston kitchen, I got busy with the grain mill that I'd clamped to a serving trolley stationed nearby. All three recipes called for very different types of grain. One wanted amber malt, another roasted barley, the third chocolate. And no two called for the same amounts. One called for two pounds, one for two and a bit, one for two pounds five ounces. I compromised with crystal malt, which usually makes for a slightly sweeter final beer. And I decided to add just over two pounds—another compromise—which I dumped into the mill and started grinding, taking care to adjust the plates so that the malt was broken up but not reduced to powder—a mess to clean up afterward. I then dumped the crystal malt into a cheesecloth bag, which I tied with a very long piece of heavy twine. When the water hit the right temperature, I tossed the bag in and put the lid on. My instructions said keep the brew at 165 degrees, which meant constantly lifting the lid to check my thermometer and turning the burner on and off. It was variously too hot or too cool. After thirty minutes, I pulled out the bag, splattering wort everywhere, and quickly tossed it in the sink.

Malt extract is amazingly viscous stuff. It's quite sweet, and it looks a lot like honey. At this point, I lifted my pot off the burner and began adding the extract, scraping it out of its tub with a rubber spatula, then dipping the tub into the hot wort to rinse out as much of the extract as possible. After this, I put the pot back on the burner and brought it to a boil. Every beer recipe seems to require that you boil it for an hour. I have no idea why. The fact that beer was boiled was why in the old days people drank it instead of water, but it would have been just as sterile after ten minutes. The bulk of my time was spent making sure the wort didn't boil over. Happily, that old wives' tale about watched pots is true.

Fifteen minutes into said hour, I dropped in my first hops. Typically, you add three lots of hops to a brew. The first infusion is called bittering hops, and they give the brew its bitter taste. The second infusion, usually done near the end of the boil, is aroma hops. The third, generally added after the wort has been taken off the heat, is the finishing hops. Part of the magic of brewing is knowing which hops to use for which purpose. For my bittering hops, I was using Fuggles, in pellet form. I love Fuggles because it sounds like a British rock band from the 1960s—Meet the Fuggles. It is a mainstay of older English brewing styles.

At the hour mark, I lifted the pot off the burner and threw in half an ounce of Goldings hops (for aroma). Then I tossed in eight ounces of demerara sugar—for a nice dark color and to give the yeast something more to work with. I put the pot by the sink, dropped in my chiller and turned on the cold water tap—at which point parts two and three of the adapter I had created blew across the room. I stuck the hose onto the tap with metal tape instead. Twenty-five minutes later, I siphoned the cooled wort into my large white plastic tub and pitched my yeast. With that, I snapped on the lid and put my air lock in place.

The kitchen looked like it had been hit with a wort bomb from twenty thousand feet. Sticky brown syrup covered every counter and had dribbled down the fronts of all the cabinets—including one, oddly, above the stove, high over my head. My shoes stuck to the floor with each step. But my work was done; now it was up to the yeast.

MILD ALE

MILD ALE IS a rich-tasting beer, dark in color, and light in hops, often made by adding sugar to the cask as it ferments. Our recipe features demerara sugar, which makes it dark. Traditional milds had quite a low alcohol content—around 3.0 to 3.5 percent alcohol by volume. It's a good example of what is called a session beer. If a group of people are going to spend an evening or a few hours after work drinking together (that is, a session), then they want a beer with a relatively low alcohol content. Mild fit that bill. It could be drunk while working, too, a more common practice in the nineteenth century.

Time was, mild ruled Britannia, or at least England and Wales, and spread throughout the Empire. (According to Brian Glover in *The Oxford Companion to Beer*, Molson was brewing it in Montreal by 1859.) Time has not been kind to mild, however. In England, after the Second World War, it came to be seen as old-fashioned, something drunk by elderly men in cloth caps while discussing their whippets' racing form.

Our version is an amalgam of three recipes we found but lacked the proper ingredients for.

GRAIN BILL

5 lbs Malt extract

2 lbs 1 oz Crystal malt

8 oz Demerara sugar

(Total 7 lbs 9 oz)

HOPS BILL

0.75 oz Fuggles (60 minutes)

0.5 oz Cascade (0 minutes)

(Note: Used pellet hops)

YEAST

One packet Lallemand Danstar

Nottingham Ale Yeast

Original gravity (OG): 1.050

Final gravity (FG): 1.010

Method: Bring 3 U.S. gallons to steeping temperature, 165–170 degrees Fahrenheit. Turn off heat and add crystal malt in a mesh bag. Steep for 30 minutes. Remove from heat, remove crystal malt, add malt extract, stir and bring to boil. At the boil, add Fuggles. Boil for 45 minutes, stir in sugar and boil for an additional 15 minutes. Irish moss and yeast nutrient could be added at this point, though we didn't. Top off with additional water in the fermenter to bring it to 5 gallons. Add dry yeast packet.

(A note on bottling: When it comes time to bottle, practice is to add ¾ cup of priming sugar, usually dextrose, dissolved in water, to kick off carbonation again. We do this by racking the beer back into the primary, adding the sugar and then bottling. For smaller quantities, the amount should be modified accordingly.)

Three

"ARE YOU SURE IT'S BARLEY?"

I WAS AT BEST a sometime farmer. That couldn't be helped. My field of barley lay almost two hours away from our Kingston house, up twisty and in places badly surfaced two-lane highways. To complicate matters further, this was the summer we decided, after years of renting it out, to sell our Toronto house. The housing market there was going insane, we heard, and it seemed foolish not to take advantage of it before the bubble burst and people came back to their senses. We had been in our house there for more than thirty years, and although we hadn't exactly kept coal in our bathtub, I do remember our daughter returning from university in Montreal and declaring that the house looked as if "it had been torn apart by drunken monkeys." We knew that we had to do a lot of work to get it ready to sell in an exacting market.

So at the beginning of July, we moved back to the city. For the next two months, we shuttled from Toronto to Kingston to the farm and then back again, often twice in the same week, in a motorized version of the old Battle of the Atlantic New York–Halifax–St. John's triangle run. This wasn't even part-time farming; it was more like farming snapshots, one brief exposure after another.

THEY TELL YOU to trail your hop vines up their lines clockwise. Mine did it of their own free will, circularly twining their way up the strings I had run from stakes to the eaves of the chicken coop. The Nugget hops were far and away doing the best, with the Willamette coming second and the Cascade bringing up the rear. I wasn't quite sure why. It might be that the Nugget had the best location, but given that all the plants were up against a white wall with a southern exposure, I don't think there could have been that much difference. Maybe Nugget was just the hardiest. Or maybe in two months they'd all be doing well.

"Are you sure it's barley?" Catharine asked, as we trudged up the driveway to check out my field on a mid-June Saturday. This had become her recurring question. And, I suppose, a legitimate one. By this point, the growth was six inches high, but there was really nothing to differentiate it from a shaggy, neglected lawn. It was completely possible that what we were looking at was whatever particular crop had been planted there before Harold had plowed the field for me. Had I tossed all that seed around for nothing?

I didn't really think so. I could see, as we walked around my field, that the growth had continued in erratic patches, only now more evident—a tuft here, a bald spot there. Rather like the hair on my own head, in fact. This suggested that it had been seeded by me, not by the hand of God.

I was worried about weeds, though. Among the patches and clumps of barley, a lot of milkweed and pigweed was coming up. In some places, the weeds were doing better than the barley. The expert opinion on barley (well, according to the book by two hippie brothers I bought about the care and maintenance of the brewer's garden) was that you don't need to weed it, because the plants grow so close together. (This was all part of the great "simplicity" myth surrounding barley.) Now, I can understand that if you were growing ten thousand acres of barley, you'd be happy to go with this assertion, but given that I had such a (relatively) small patch, I thought I might as well do some weeding. And although there was some question about whether the green, grass-like plant I had in my field was barley, there was no mistaking the weeds. They looked like weeds.

In some ways, what I was doing was closer to lawn care than farming. Equipped with one of those short little tools you use to dig weeds out of a lawn and a green plastic milk crate, I got to work. Taking pains not to step on the barley (stupid, if in the process of saving it, I destroyed it), I began working through the field width-wise. I'd shift my milk crate, bend, push the forked tip of the weeder deep into the soil and lever out a weed, or more often weeds, and drop it in my carton. I'd straighten up, spot the next weed and move my carton. As I rooted out the weeds, I noticed that although the surface of the field may have been drier than before, four or five inches down it was still damp. Over the weekend, from my three thousand square feet of barley, I dug out five milk crates full of compacted weeds. I could have taken out a few more, but my enthusiasm ran out well before the weeds did. Some of the weeds seemed to be invading from the edges; but I suspected that others had been in the manure I used. *Too bad,* I remember thinking, *I can't make weed beer. I'd dominate the market.*

My barley was weed-infested, but it seemed to be doing fine overall. The hops, however, had wilt. Wilt is one of those things that can survive for years in the soil, and some strains of hop are particularly susceptible to it. It can completely destroy German Hallertauer, a popular hop used to make lager. I noticed that my middle guys, the Cascade, really seemed to be struggling. I could see the progressive march of the disease up the vines—the leaves at the bottom were yellowy brown, dry and dead; those a foot or so up were drooping, their robust green color draining away; those higher up again were beginning to shrivel at the edges. One of the keys to getting a lot of hop growth is to trim any extra shoots and to cut away a lot of the bottom leaves. This technique helps with wilt, too. I pinched off the affected leaves, and a few more healthy ones while I was at it, as a sort of insurance policy, and tossed them far, far away from my plants. After that, I sprayed the leaves with a baking soda mixture and "manure tea"—what you get if you leave manure to steep in a bucket of water, then siphon off the all-too-evocative yellowish-brown liquid.

These old-time remedies also fight wilt. The manure tea, alas, led to pointed questions around the farm's dining room table when I fail to remove the bucket from the coopio, which is not well ventilated.

As I worked, I conceded that even without wilt, the hops were going to be a particular challenge. If I really was going to brew beer completely from scratch over the winter, I needed enough hops of my own. Given ideal climate, soil and other conditions, a single plant can produce up to two and a half pounds of cones, while they lose a fair bit of weight when you dry them, a single plant should produce enough hops for several batches of beer. But my problem was that hops really only get going in their third year. In their first year, the plants concentrate on putting down strong root systems. They do produce cones, just not a lot. For my scheme to work, I needed almost all the plants to pull through.

And wilt aside, I could see that some of the plants were doing fairly well. My star, Nugget, was six feet high by this point. Others were well up over the two-foot-high chicken-wire cages I had built around them to keep out pests. But two of them looked dead. I decided to clip these right down. If they were dead, they would still be dead. If there was some life left, they might bounce back.

BY MID-JULY, the barley was doing well, a lovely field of light blue-green grain that shimmered in the wind and stood out in a nice contrast to the stubbly brown grasses around it. The barley was sprouting its trademark "beard"—the fringy bit at the top that you always see featured on beer labels or boxes of cereal. There would be no more questions about whether I was growing barley or grass. The beards clinched it.

There were plenty of weeds mixed in with the barley, but I decided not to bother with them. Over the past few weeks, since the first time I had ventured into the fields with weeding implement in hand, I had taken out several additional milk cartons stuffed with weeds, but I am not sure that it made much difference. The weeds came back, but the barley kept growing. Ecological equilibrium, I guess.

The hops that I had trimmed right back had survived and were sending out new sprouts, though they probably wouldn't end up producing much. The ones that had been badly hit with wilt seemed to have benefited from the baking powder and manure tea sprays, and were sprouting healthy, attractive leaves and tendrils. So attractive that I now faced another problem: Japanese beetles. One of the hardest hop pests to deal with, these compact green beetles had chewed great holes in the hop leaves and were getting busy on my nascent cones, too. Trundling out the extension ladder once again, I quickly disposed of these guys by flicking them with my thumb and forefinger into a jar filled with soapy water.

Afterward, while rummaging around in the chicken coop, I noticed a plastic bottle full of murky red fluid. Two of the other farm members—I'll call them the lawyer and the chef—had a vegetable garden going, and I had seen them using this organic insecticide, which they had made themselves. I sprayed it on the leaves of my hops to stop the beetles from coming back. The next morning when I checked them, I almost had a heart attack. The plants were drooping badly. I noticed that the afflicted areas seemed to correspond exactly with where I had sprayed. It was my turn for pointed questions. It turned out that one of the ingredients in the spray was supposed to be crushed chilies. They had used commercial chili pepper, which contains salt. I had covered the leaves of my precious hops in a fine film of salt, and the sun had done the rest.

I snipped away the damaged leaves and the plants shook it off. But I felt like the disasters never stopped. If the hops weren't wilting, they were being eaten by beetles. Kill the beetles and the next thing you knew the leaves were covered with tiny caterpillars. I got rid of them, only to turn a leaf over one morning and be confronted by a creature the size and shape of a scrubbing brush—a red, black and yellow upside-down scrubbing brush.

Whenever you read about Buddha or St. Francis of Assisi, people always go on about their respect for every living thing. This, it seems to me, is the attitude of someone who never had to deal personally with goutweed or an aphid infestation. Those problems were "out there" for them, a question of attitude, not reality. For those of us on the front lines of gardening and farming, reality is very different. That bright, gaudy caterpillar on the underside of a hop leaf is your archenemy, a selfish freeloader who is robbing you blind. Sacred? Yeah, pal, I got your sacred. (*Fires away with organic bug spray.*) Right here.

I PULLED THE thick black hose over my shoulder and coiled it once around me. Leaning into the hose with my shoulder, I began tugging its long, trailing length behind me, up the sloping hill, past our pond and between two small clumps of willowy trees, in the direction of my barley.

It's odd about weather. If you live in a city, and I have lived in cities my whole life, the definition of good weather, especially in the summer, is dry and hot. The lack of rain only becomes an issue when the city starts telling people to stop watering their lawns. Get out in the countryside, though, and everything changes. If you are trying to grow something, rainy days are suddenly important and a long, unbroken string of hot, sunny days, an alarming prospect. I could imagine a farmer looking out of his window at a succession of such days and slipping ever deeper into a gloomy personal depression. *More bad weather,* he'd think. You don't want to keep on the sunny side. You want to keep on the rainy side.

We'd been blessed with a wet spring—almost too wet, in fact. The wet weather had dragged on. *June 22,* I wrote in my journal, *it is raining, a nice, slow steady rain... June 23, rained again in the night—an inundation that had me convinced in my sleepy state that the hose to the dishwasher had burst... July 18, rained while I was barbecuing, of course, and then during the night twice. Dumped a lot.*

Late in July, the weather began to change. It simply got too damn hot. At the end of one particularly brutal week, when the temperatures at the farm had hit thirty-five degrees, I could feel, almost see, the heat radiating up at me from the dry, hard soil. I had planted my field so that it sloped slightly downhill—actually, in two directions, lengthwise from right to left and widthwise from back to front. I hoped the slope would help it to drain. But now I saw that the gently sloping hill's southern orientation had the particularly nasty effect of tipping my barley to take the fullest brunt of the sun's rays. Some of the shoots planted in the lowest part of my field had died. In other surviving patches, I could see brown creeping up the stalks. Certain doubters thought I wouldn't have enough.

Now, of course, from what I'd read, barley doesn't need to be watered. Any more than it needs to be weeded. But I had to get water to it. Exactly how I wasn't sure. We have a very nice pond between my field and the farmhouse, and I thought maybe that would be a source. But it was just Catharine and I on the farm that weekend, and a two-person bucket brigade, where you're looking at carrying each pail seventy-five or more feet, isn't all that effective.

Not for the first time, I found myself in that netherworld between agriculture and lawn maintenance. The farmhouse is surrounded by fairly large lawns. On either side of the building sits one of those reels on wheels that hold about fifty feet of hose. If I could hook them together, I might be able to reach the barley. I took the hoses off the two reels, found a third in the basement and a fourth hanging coiled on a nail on a wall of the henhouse. Screwing them all together gave me about two hundred feet of hose, to which I attached a lawn sprinkler. With this I could pretty much water all my barley.

Our biggest concern was the pump that brings water up to the house from the well. Another two hundred feet uphill was a hell of distance for it to pump. When I opened the outside tap for the first time, I could hear the pump straining away in the cellar. To make sure we didn't burn it out, we agreed I should turn it off every half hour or so. So I'd turn on the hose, then trot up the path to my field and pull the spraying sprinkler into place, taking care not to crush too much of my barley. Then I set the timer on my watch for twenty minutes. I had estimated that if I wanted to water the whole patch before the day's end, that was how often I would have to shift the sprinkler, given the radius it covered. Back in the house, I set the timer on the stove for thirty minutes. At my watch's beep at the twenty-minute mark, I ran up the hill and dragged the sprinkler to a new spot. By the time I was back in the farmhouse, the thirty-minute warning was sounding on the stove timer, so I thumped down the basement stairs, turned off the pump at the circuit breaker and waited a minute or two. After I flicked the breaker back on, I ran up the stairs and reset the stove timer. Then it was out the front door, down the steps and back to the barley. Planting, weeding, watering—there is a lot of repetition in farming. When it's going well, I think it becomes rhythmic—you get into a groove and zone out a little. Often, though, it's just assembly-line work—only in nicer surroundings.

It took all afternoon, but I managed to water every part of my barley patch. I didn't know if it would help. It needed a serious soaking rain. But if frenetic energy combined with personal anxiety could make the difference, my crop had nothing to worry about.

"NOW ON TO Essex County. Ralph, apologies for last week. Yes, I did fail to mention that a copper solution used on winter alfalfa can also boost productivity..."

I was lying on the carpeted floor of my office in our Toronto house, listening on my phone to the recorded weekly update by Peter Johnson, the cereal guy with the Ontario Ministry of Agriculture. I generally work standing up, but if I have to sit on hold or listen to a long recorded message, I find it's often more comfortable to just lie down and let it wash over me. I was playing hooky from installing a shelving unit in the walk-in closet, all part of the presale house fluffing.

I was worried about when my barley would finally be ready to harvest. It looked like it might be right around the week when I was supposed to be working at Lake of Bays Brewing. The previous fall, I had spent part of the Thanksgiving weekend signing books at Lake of Bays, a craft brewery that had opened only months before in the Muskoka hamlet of Baysville. The young founder, Darren Smith, had given Catharine and me a tour of his brewery, and I had been impressed by his enthusiasm and, even more, his knowledge. A subsequent encounter with him and some of his crew at a pub in Bracebridge had planted the idea that he might be someone to spend time with. We'd fixed it up so that I could work at his brewery while staying at my sisters' nearby cottage.

But if harvest time coincided with my Lake of Bays week, it would mean a hasty three-hour drive through Algonquin Park to the farm. I knew about how long the barley was supposed to take to mature—ninety days. But that is very approximate—the weather, the soil and the climate play their parts. What's true for North Dakota isn't true for eastern Ontario. My hope was that I'd be able to let the barley go a bit longer than ninety days, to give me a little slack time. But I quickly learned that no online source, including agricultural colleges and government entities, would come out and say whether I could take that gamble. The Ontario agriculture ministry site alluded to a slack time—but totally relationally: Newdale barley took two days longer than (oh, I don't know) Bentley, which in turn took less time than Bornholm, which took a week longer than HY 435-2R. Following this reasoning, your only hope would be to drive around until you saw someone harvesting a field planted with the barley that matured just before yours.

That's why I had called Peter. He was out in the field—literally, I mean—but after listening to the message he'd left on his machine, I phoned in to the province's crop hotline. This service consisted of him reporting on all the grains right across the province, based on people's first-person reports to him. It had an incredibly intimate feel to it, like listening in on a party line, with plenty of shout-outs (if an ag rep can shout out) to people across the province. On and on it went, crop after crop, county by county. But nothing about Newdale. I hung up when he got to dwarf bunt.

I decided to check the seed company's website for information on Newdale's maturation. There it was: "mid." *Mid* what? The woman who answered the phone when I called referred me to the eastern Ontario rep. I had, he told me, at least three weeks to go.

"Don't rush it," he said.

"YOU'D BETTER HEAD over to Grey County."

Catharine and I were on the road, again, heading north to the farm on a Saturday morning in early August. We'd taken off early, if not bright.

We had the radio tuned to the local community station, to the Polish show to be exact, which featured performers from the western edge of the valley. I liked it, though I have to admit that apart from the performers' names (including the memorable Donny "Fiddle Fingers" Palubeskie), it sounded just like the Scottish, Irish and French shows: rapid-fire jigs and polkas sawed out on violins.

We were sharing the car that morning with an elephant. A blue-green, bearded, two-rowed elephant that had been dogging me, unacknowledged, for a few weeks. My barley had been doing well until the great blast of heat hit us in late July. Catharine believed, and I was willing, grudgingly, to accept that she might be right, that I would need to find barley from somewhere else.

Grey County was her idea. That's where they grow most of the barley in Ontario. "See if you can figure out who can get it for you there," she suggested.

"There are people who grow it in Prince Edward," I said. "I've got the name of a guy down there."

"If you go to Grey you can stay with your cousin."

"Prince Edward is closer." Grey County lies south of Georgian Bay and west of Algonquin Park, a good four-hour drive from home.

"It's too hot and humid for barley in Prince Edward. You said so yourself."

"Yes, but not everywhere. This guy does it successfully."

"But if you—" and then she stopped. "This," she said, "is an argument only a married couple could have."

I agreed, for the public record, to go to Grey. Secretly, however, I believed my barley won't fail me.

SOME BEERS WERE for learning; some beers were for drinking; some beers were, in the words of Monty Python, "for laying down and avoiding." This one definitely fell into the second category. We referred to it as our bière ordinaire, and its purpose was to ensure we had something to drink while carrying out our various brewing experiments.

The basis of this brew was pale malt extract, after which we tossed in everything but the kitchen sink: the recipe below calls for some two-row barley, but in fact it was mostly two row, along with whatever tiny amounts of other malt I had sitting around. We also added crystal malt, roasted barley, oatmeal, brown sugar and demerara sugar. Catharine hovered over the brew with a shoe at one point, but I waved her off.

In terms of hops, by this point we had moved past pellets to freeze-dried. The major lesson with this recipe was you can put pretty much anything into a beer and it should work. In fact, this mishmash tasted great. The only problem was we didn't take an accurate reading of the original gravity, so to this day I have no idea of the alcohol content.

GRAIN BILL

7.5 lbs Pale malt extract
14 oz Mystery mix (mostly pale)
24 oz Crystal malt
2 oz Roasted barley
10 oz Brown sugar
8 oz Large flake oatmeal
10 oz Demerara sugar
(Total 11 lbs 12 oz)

HOPS

0.75 oz Cascade (45 minutes)
0.5 oz Fuggles (15 minutes)

YEAST

Lallemand Danstar Nottingham Ale Yeast (recycled from previous brew)
OG: Unknown
FG: 1.012

Method: Heat 1.5 U.S. gallons of water to 170 degrees Fahrenheit. Add grain bag filled with barley and oatmeal and steep for 30 minutes. Sparge grains at 168 degrees Fahrenheit, bringing volume up to 2 gallons. (Sparging is pouring additional water over the grain after the wort has been poured off.) Add malt extract, both sugars and water to make 6 gallons. Boil for 60 minutes, adding hops as indicated. Remove from heat. Bring the total volume to 5 gallons. Strain. Cool to 70 degrees Fahrenheit and pitch (that is, add) yeast. Rack to secondary fermenter when gravity is stable. Prime, bottle and age at room temperature at least 2 weeks before chilling.

Four

IT'S ALL ABOUT THE HOSES

MY SISTER SALLY'S Volkswagen camper van crunched into the gravel parking lot of the Lake of Bays Brewing Company a little before eight in the morning. Elaine, the woman working in the store attached to the brewery, told me that Darren wasn't there yet, so we walked over to get coffee with her at the local café. Darren showed up soon afterward.

"So, you're with us for three days," he said. Someone else had made the same comment. Confused, I explained that, no, I planned to be there all week. It was an awkward moment. Wherever, I wondered, had they got that idea? (Later, I realized: from me. At first I had said three days—I think because that was how long I was planning to spend working at another brewery. Then I got it into my head that a week at Lake of Bays would be much better—without bothering to tell Darren. I guess my attitude was: Why should I? I knew how long I was going to be there.)

He handed me a pair of steel-toed rubber boots and introduced me to the guys I would be working with the most, Mark Campbell and Mike Pawlick, students from the new brewing program at Niagara College, near Niagara Falls, who were on a work placement. We were soon joined by another young guy, Matt. Noticing that everyone I would be working with had a name that started with M (later, I would meet Mitch, the sales manager), I told people to call me "Mian."

Brewing doesn't generally produce child prodigies, but I think Darren comes close. Slight and blond, he could be thought of as the Mozart of craft brewing. A dedicated home brewer, Darren had dreamed of opening his own microbrewery while he was still an undergraduate studying commerce at Montreal's McGill University—without any very clear idea of how to go about it, as he said himself. By coincidence, in 2007 his father had bought the site of a defunct lumberyard in Baysville, a town of about 350 souls that caters to the summer people whose cottages line the shores of Lake of Bays—without any very clear idea of what to do with it. Son's nebulous idea for a brewery met the father's nebulous idea for an investment and the Lake of Bays brewing company was born—housed, just to keep things in the family, in a new building designed by Darren's sister, an architect. The brewery opened on the May long weekend in 2010, when Darren was twenty-three years old. The company initially offered just one beer, a pale ale, but by the time I showed up, it had added a second, a darker beer known as a rousse, and employed more than fifteen people. This made it, I would guess, the town's largest employer. (And a highly visible one—just a few weeks before, Darren and his crew had dumped an unsatisfactory brew down the drain, overwhelming the town's sewage treatment plant and causing beer to bubble out of people's drains.)

The brewery proper was painted amber and white, the company's colors (and, I later realized, the color of beer), and featured a row of tall windows along one side, which lets staff work to a great degree by natural light—and gives passersby a glimpse of Lake of Bays' brewing operations. The company store, where you can buy beer and branded shirts and caps, is built into one corner of the building. Outside stands a large circular malt hopper made of corrugated metal and covered with hop vines, which were just sprouting their cones the week I was there. This filled me with angst about my own hops and their struggles with bugs, blights and inappropriately formulated sprays. Next to the brewery stands a two-story building (or strictly, buildings, though they have been melded into a single rambling structure) that came with the property. The downstairs is used for storage; the upstairs houses the brewery's business offices, a series of odd rooms run together higgledy-piggledy and featuring floors at odd different heights and doors punched through from one building to another. The structure presents a shabby contrast to the shiny new brewery, but the Lake of Bays Brewing Company has been growing too fast to fret about superficial stuff.

IT'S ALL ABOUT THE HOSES

I'd been worried that I would be a bit of a fifth wheel. It turned out, however, that it was lucky I was there. Mike had slashed his hand on some broken glass the previous week, an occupational hazard of the beer-making biz, and in his case severely enough to need stitches. I would be doing the work that, for the time being, he couldn't.

This first morning, we were going to be bottling. Not terribly relevant from my point of view, but I was eager to help. The bottling line was at the back of the plant, tucked between the cold room and a large stainless steel fermentation tank. First thing, we wheeled a skid of bottles into place. To my untrained eye, this job looked pretty precarious: the bottles were stacked upright on it, probably five feet high, with each layer resting on a sheet of heavy brown cardboard and the whole shebang shrink-wrapped together. Because there was nothing else holding the bottles in place, you had to be really careful as you unwrapped the skid not to tap or hit them. We did manage to drop a few.

Anyway, Mark would grab a bunch of these bottles, slap them into a holder which allowed him to flip them over, and then put them onto a tray that squirted water up into each one individually to clean them. From there, he put the bottles onto a flat metal table, where they were fed into a device that stuck a tube into them six at a time, kicking up a beery mist and making a satisfying *thunk*. This step shot a uniform amount of beer into each bottle (uniform, that is, if and only if the pressure in the tank in the nearby cold room was maintained, something that got overlooked the first morning I was there). Another *thunk,* and the bottles were capped. Then they slid out the other side of this contraption, and when enough of them had accumulated, a whole row would be pushed onto a tiny conveyor belt and caught by a strange corkscrew device that propelled them through a label attacher. (We spent a fair bit of the morning trying to get the attacher to [a] to actually apply labels to bottles and [b] not to instead spit out gummy labels whenever it felt like it, which we then had to frantically peel off the moving parts of the bottler before they jammed it.)

My job? Simplicity itself. Kenzie, the teenaged girl working there for the summer, would fill the six-packs and then hand them over to me. My task was to close the box, which required me to make two folds, then flip it over and stamp it with its best-before date: January 8, 2012. I was doing all right on the whole two folds thing, but, to be honest, my date stamping was shaky. Most of my boxes said, to eyes not trained to decipher smeared ink, "Best Before: January 8, 2012." Then I tossed the box on to Matt, who was dropping them into flats of twenty-four, which he put on a skid when they were filled. We'd filled the better part of a skid, the morning's work, before I was sending a clear message in the best-before department.

But that was a minor triumph. When I started off, Kenzie was just one six-pack ahead of me. After an hour or two, she was two ahead, then three. This was venturing into *I Love Lucy* territory, the episode where Lucy goes to work in the bonbon factory—fall any further behind and I'd have to start stuffing bottles into my pockets, then drinking them as fast as possible.

There was a hypnotic quality to the whole process. Here comes the six-pack. Make a fold, make another fold, flip it, stamp it. Hand it on. The radio was tuned to the local "music of your life" station, and I was half-listening over the hissing and clinking sounds of the machine that fills the bottles when Bruce Springsteen's "Glory Days" came on. I'm no big fan of the Boss, but this was one of those moments when a song and your situation match perfectly. "Glory days," he sang. (Fold, fold, flip, stamp.) "Well, they'll pass you by." (Fold, fold, flip, stamp.) "Glory days." *Always wanted out of this town,* I thought to myself. (Fold, fold, flip, stamp.). *Would have left, if I hadn't knocked up my girlfriend the night of the prom.* (Fold, fold, flip, stamp.) *Now I'm trapped on this dead-end bottling line.* (Fold, fold, flip, stamp.) At that moment, I wasn't listening to a Bruce Springsteen song, I wasn't even in a Bruce Springsteen song—I *was* a Bruce Springsteen song. I could see my beat-up car, my shabby bungalow with the dying lawn—and see them so completely that I didn't notice that the soggy labels had jammed the bottling machine and the bottles were beginning to back up and wobble precariously on the edge of the conveyor belt.

In the end, we filled five skids. There are 264 bottles in a layer and each skid holds five layers, so that works out to 6,600 bottles. That's a pretty typical run, though the week before, they had set a new record: 8,800 plus in a single bottling run. Just four people filling boxes six at a time. Patrick, the plant manager who'd somehow found his way from his native South Africa to Muskoka, called it soul-destroying work—particularly the handstamping thing, which they were getting ready to replace while I was there. Their "problem," if you can call it that, is one that seems to be afflicting the craft brewing industry worldwide. Lake of Bays Brewing was growing so fast—faster, I suspect, than they expected—that their equipment and their people could barely keep up. (By 2013, they were producing four times as much beer in the average week.)

It was surprising to discover just how physical commercial beer making was, particularly small-scale craft brewing. There was a lot of hefting and turning involved in bottling (excellent, I told myself, for the obliques), but it was positively futuristic compared to kegging. Later that week, we spent a morning filling five-liter kegs with rousse. We'd stick a hose into a metal can, fill it, then slap on a plastic top that featured a built-in pump and spout. A darker, though not really dark, beer, rousse isn't seen much in Ontario, though it has a following, a drinkership, you might say, in Quebec. I was a bit cool to this flavor before. I got why they made it—the pale ale hit the drinkers who wanted a lighter-colored, smoother beer; the rousse got those people whose tastes ran to darker drinks such as stouts and porters. But filling these finicky cans by hand put me right off it. It wasn't the amount of beer on my hands and arms that did me in or watching it bubble up over my work boots. Oh no, much worse. We put the cans on the floor to fill them. I sat on a small cart, with a cardboard box as a cushion. But there was so much beer dribbling everywhere (Mark was filling sitting beside me) that after an hour or so I started to get a distinct impression of dampness around where I sat—spilled rousse had seeped under the cardboard and was now being soaked up by my shorts.

Beer should never be taken rectally.

IT'S ALL ABOUT THE HOSES

THE MORNING WAS largely overcast, what little sun there was glittering off the small waves on the large gray lake. The mighty nine-horsepower engine on the Coutts family's cedar runabout droned on and on. Off to my right, I passed a dark, humpbacked island.

In the course of my working life I have commuted by subway, streetcar and, during a memorable year when I lived in London, double-decker bus, as well as on foot and bicycle. But I don't think anything can match commuting by small boat on a large lake. You've got scenery; you've got your personal space. You don't have silence, that's true, but you're no mere passenger, you're your own master and commander.

There aren't many people around on a Muskoka lake midweek. That's a good thing, actually. You need a license to operate even a tiny powerboat like my family's. I do have a license—or to be more specific, bits and pieces of one stuffed in a desk drawer somewhere. I got it more than a decade ago, and time has not been kind to it. Apparently, the police do stop people, and they will issue fines, but I was pretty sure that before eight in the morning, the police boat would be sitting on its trailer in the Tim Hortons parking lot in Bracebridge while its crew downed their morning double-doubles.

Where the lake narrowed down into the South Muskoka River, I twisted back on the throttle and dropped my speed, moving past grand two-story boathouses boasting cupolas and copper weather vanes. I wondered about the "cottages" hidden in the trees behind them. Coming in alongside the old steamboat dock in Baysville with its covered landing stage, I pushed the engine into neutral and let the runabout glide in. I had to hurry. It was almost eight, and I didn't want to be late for my first day of real beer making—as opposed to filling, stamping and folding—at Lake of Bays Brewing.

We were going to be making rousse. Yesterday, at the end of the day, I had helped measure out the malt and the hops for today's brewing, working from an ingenious spreadsheet. Lake of Bays had lost its original brewmaster in the spring. "Creative differences," I gathered. Darren had found a replacement who would be joining them soon, but in the meantime these spreadsheets, which listed ingredients, times, temperatures and the desired results for the various tests they carried out during brewing, let any reasonably attentive person carry out successful brewing. In the cold room, we had opened various heavy foil bags filled with hops and dumped them into plastic bins, which we then marked RO1, RO2, RO3. This was the sequence we'd add them in. Not for the first time, I was struck by the strangeness of hops. Pungent? Visceral? Extenuating? I can't put my finger on something that is as much felt as smelt. People sometimes talk of a nonmystical "sixth" sense called umami. I wonder if hops don't point toward a seventh—something between taste and smell and touch, which also, I swear, involves the eyes but not in a visual sense.

I was going to be working with Darren himself today. Later in the week, I would make pale ale with Chris, a university pal of Darren's who had been Lake of Bays' first hire. Their styles differed. Darren was intense, Chris a little more relaxed—not sloppy (in fact, it had been Chris who had developed the complex spreadsheets that we followed to brew), just a little more laid back. But in general, although we brewed very different beers, the procedures were very similar.

Beer making happens in the brewhouse. "Well, *perforce*," I hear you say. This isn't a separate building, although I imagine that once, very long ago, it was. I can't speak for the setup at giant commercial breweries, but at Lake of Bays, the house, if you will, consisted of four large stainless steel tanks, three of which had hatches in the top, the sort of thing you might imagine on a submarine. The capacity of the tanks in the Lake of Bays brewhouse is half that of their fermentation tanks. So when they brew, they have to go through the entire process twice to fill the fermentation tanks.

The brewing tanks were arranged two to a side of a metal catwalk that stood about five feet off the concrete floor. The liquor tank (not booze but hot water, which in brewing is referred to as liquor) and the lauter tun—the big tank where the mash was first mixed—were on one side of the catwalk, the kettle and the whirlpool on the other. The equipment at Lake of Bays is state of the art—at the far end of the catwalk was a touch-activated computer screen. If you pressed any listing on a menu down the side, some part of the brewhouse would display, showing whether this pump or that was on or off, what the temperature of the water was and so forth.

One of my first jobs would be to feed the specialty grains into the mill, which was kept in a small room on the ground floor tucked between two fermentation tanks. I had thought that the big corrugated hopper outside the brewery was strictly a gimmick. Not so. In fact, it held pale malted two-row barley. This malt was the basis of all the beers that Lake of Bays brewed: the two regular ones and their seasonal specialties. I later learned that this malt was their own specific blend of two row, created out of different malted barleys for them by their malting company. This hopper fed directly into the mill.

But the mill was used to grind more than just pale two-row malt. A lot of the difference among beers comes from the specialty malts—a crystal malt, say, or a dark roasted one—that go into the brew. Some brews use other grains, such as malted wheat or rye. Set out by weight and type in a list called the "grain bill," these varying ingredients help determine a beer's flavor, aroma, color and even its ineffable "mouth feel." If you think of that pale two-row malt as the bass line or drumbeat of a beer, the specialty malts and grains provide the guitar solo or the piccolo.

The grains I was grinding now would be part of the afternoon's brew. I weighed out two different types of specialty malt in their bags on a scale. Once I knew I had the right amount, I boosted each bag up and over my shoulder and then dumped it into the hopper. The grain tends to stick to the hopper's sides, though, so I needed to reach in and push it down with my fingers. But not too far—there's no market for finger beer. The mill was connected to a long tube that ran out of the room and along the ceiling of the brewery. The flick of a switch started an auger turning in the pipe that carried the ground malt up and high over the brewhouse, ultimately dropping it into another hopper, this one suspended over the lauter tun.

Darren pushed a switch and started water running into the lauter tun. One hundred liters to begin. Then we tossed in a tub-full of calcium chloride tablets. People tend to think of craft brewers as using traditional or pure ingredients, so this "additive" might surprise them. But it is quite common and in its own way very traditional. Hard water—water with lots of dissolved minerals in it—brings out the flavor of hops, something that British brewers in Burton-on-Trent discovered long ago when they began using water drawn from deep artesian wells to brew their famous pale ale. The local water that Lake of Bays Brewing draws on is very soft, so it really needs the tablets for the beer to work. We tested the water's pH to make sure the calcium chloride hadn't made it too alkaline, which would affect its flavor.

The next step was to pull open the gate on the bottom of the wide-diameter tube hanging down from the hopper, releasing the grain. It poured into a square gray device called a grist hydrator, which wet the grain somewhat and then dropped it into the lauter tun.

My big job was to play with a very annoying tap that controlled the flow of water into the lauter tun. You want to fill the lauter tun as quickly as possible but only at a certain temperature. Increase the flow too much, and the temperature started to drop. Correct for that, and the flow began to decrease. I had a big round dial in front of me, about the only nondigital measuring device in the brewhouse, that I watched intently, twisting the tap first this way, then that to keep the water flowing in at a consistent 170 degrees Fahrenheit. While I was busy with this, Darren started the rakes rotating inside the tun. These mix together the water and the grain, a process known as mashing in. I'd done the same thing at home by stirring a wooden spoon around in my enameled pot.

Standing with one hand on the tap watching an enormous dial, fussing constantly to make sure that the temperature never wavered from the ideal, was a pleasantly absurd duty, like something out of Chaplin's *Modern Times* or Fritz Lang's *Metropolis,* and one well suited to a somewhat obsessive individual like me (mentally repeating "Zulu as Kono" before charging up any flight of stairs, thinking daily of the royal family). But it was also a key part of the brewing process.

When that water hits the relatively cooler grain, the temperature drops. That's all right, but you don't want it to drop too far, or for too long. You want it to stabilize between 150 and 160 degrees Fahrenheit. At these temperatures, the enzymes in the malt are activated and begin converting the malt's starches to sugars. These are what the yeast will later convert into alcohol. Miss that sweet spot, go too cool or too hot, and you will affect the conversion. The method we followed to add the water to the grains while maintaining a constant temperature is what's known as a single infusion. Other brewers prefer a technique called a step infusion, where the temperature is raised by successive increments to convert as many starches as possible.

Once all the water was added, I dipped a ladle into the open hatch of the lauter tun and poured some of the wort into a beaker. I put the beaker on a small white plate kept for the purpose on the table next to the stairs to the brewhouse. I squeezed an eyedropper full of brown iodine into the beaker. If the conversion was incomplete, the iodine would turn purple-black. It did not. All the starches had been converted.

With that confirmation, the wort was ready to be pumped to the kettle. Darren sent me under the catwalk to flick a valve that circulated the wort, pumping it out of the tun and then back in again—a process known as *verlaufing*, which helps extract more of the sugars in the mash. Verlaufing also helps the grain settle in the bottom of the mash tun without becoming compacted. If you get that, you have what is known as a "stuck mash," and the wort will not drain through this decidedly nonporous mess. Then, turning another valve, I started the wort on its way to the kettle, while Darren sprayed hot water into the tun to "sparge" the grain that stayed behind. Sparging ekes yet more sugars out of the mash.

The kettle is where the brewer brings the wort to the boiling point. Lake of Bays' particular kettle had three heaters built into its side at varying heights. As the level of the wort rose, we turned on successive heaters. However, the solenoids that turned on the heaters didn't always work. Mark went round to the outside of the kettle and banged on the pipes with a large rubber mallet while I listened for the telltale sign of the heaters kicking in, a satisfying *ba-woom* sound.

We wanted to fill the kettle to twenty-seven hectoliters, or just over 713 U.S. gallons, which we measured using a nifty stainless steel dipstick. When we hit the mark, we turned off the pumps and let the temperature climb. When the wort hit the boil, we pitched the first hops. As we dumped in the pellets, Darren grabbed a hose and sprayed the wort to stop it from bubbling up out of the kettle. (Later, working with Matt, I managed to distract him with a question at a key moment. Over his shoulder, I saw brown foam bubbling out of the open lid and spilling onto the brewhouse walkway. The kettle had boiled over.)

There's a lot of hurry up and wait to brewing. Since this stage—the boil—takes an hour, we turned our attention to the many other tasks that always need doing.

Foremost among these was emptying the lauter tun. The liquid wort just runs out. But the mash, that conglomeration of used-up grains... ah, the mash is another question. Darren turned a large green wheel on the side of the tun, which opened a gate in the bottom, and the mash began spilling into a big gray metal hopper. We didn't want it to plug the gate, so we each grabbed a shovel and started pulling the sodden grain toward us. Darren had asked me to set up four large plastic barrels on a skid and we shoveled the mash into these, scooping it up, pivoting, dumping and then turning back to repeat the cycle. My obliques, already worked by yesterday's efforts, were being honed to competition level. We moved just under a ton in this fashion, Darren triumphantly striking the classic muscle guy pose when we'd finished. (Later in the week, I unloaded just over a ton all by myself.) After this, I got a hose and sprayed up into the mash tun to wash out more grain. The concrete floor for about twenty feet around the tun was slick with wort and grain.

By this point, about forty-five minutes into the boil, it was time to pitch the aroma hops. Generally, we added three portions of hops to the wort when we were brewing.

First were the bittering hops, added early in the process. This first infusion gives beer a bitter flavor, via resins in the hops, but not much more; the oils that provide the aroma and more delicate elements of hops flavor are destroyed by the long boil. That's why the second batch, the aroma hops, go in near the end of the boil. Not long after this, right near the end, we dumped in the third lot, the so-called finishing hops, which would impart even more aroma. Brewers sometimes also dry-hop—add hops to the wort when it's fermenting. With no heat to drive off the oils, this boosts both the bitterness and the flavor notes from the hops. I later used the technique at home to get my beer closer to the feel of an "extreme" West Coast–style pale ale.

After the third hops infusion, we added something called Irish moss, actually dried seaweed, which helps the sediment in the wort settle out. That's a move I rarely, if ever, bothered with when brewing at home. When the boil was over, we pumped the wort into the third and final tank it would occupy in the brewhouse. Called the whirlpool, it is pretty much what the name suggests. The wort was whipped around and around, causing any leftover bits of hops or fragments of grain to settle in the middle of the tank. The clearer wort then ran through a heat exchanger, which cooled the still very hot fluid to about seventy-one degrees Fahrenheit.

Hoses. It's all about hoses, this beer business. When the beer left the inverter, it traveled through a hose snaking along the floor to what, to me, resembled a standard beer keg. It attached to the keg's top with a coupling. Another hose ran out the bottom. Earlier in the day, this keg had been filled with yeast drawn off one of the fermenting vessels. As the wort moved through the keg, it mixed with the yeast—the larger-scale version of pitching the little packet of yeast. The bottom hose carried the now-yeasty wort to one of the stainless steel fermenting tanks ranged along the wall about twenty feet from the brewhouse. Tired but content with my role—particularly my precision work on the big tap—I headed home.

When I came in the next morning, I noticed a smaller plastic hose running from the fermenter to a large plastic pail filled with water. The water was foaming frantically as carbon dioxide bubbled off the wort—fermentation was in full force. Placing the end of the hose in water ensured that while that gas was carried off the wort, no outside air—nor the contaminants it carried—could go back up into the fermentation tank. Again, it was the big-scale version of the little plastic air lock filled with water that I bunged into the lid of my plastic pail at home.

The beer would stay here for a week or so. Then it would be chilled even more—"crashed" is the technical term—and then strained through an incredible filter that resembled nothing so much as five feet of acoustic ceiling tiles clamped together in an enormous vise that was tightened by turning a gargantuan wheel. It looked like the sort of thing that Moe used to squash Larry's or Curly's head in the Three Stooges, and whenever I saw it, I mentally went "Nyong, nyong, nyong." Brewers have these nifty glass attachments that can fit onto the end of a hose and let them see the beer as it flows through. There was one fitted on the hose leading into this contraption and one on the hose leading out. Through them I could see that the beer going into the filter was milky; the beer flowing out, absolutely clear. From the filter it was pumped to one of the bright tanks (named for the filtered or "bright" beer they contain). Finally, the beer would be bottled or kegged—taking me back to where I entered the cycle my first day. And so it goes, twice a week all summer, once a week during the winter.

I came away from my week at Lake of Bays with two things. One was a case of pale ale. The other was the realization that beer making, like the rest of the food industry, is as much about cleanliness as it is about technique or finished product. We flushed hoses, we cycled acid and sterilizing fluids through brewing vats, we spritzed everything with sanitizer. The cleaning seemed central, the beer almost peripheral. But as Darren said, "You need that, to be consistent." It's an important message, but I suspect it's one that amateur brewers sometimes don't get. Again and again, you'll hear somebody say that they tried making beer and it worked really well the first few times, but after that something seemed to go wrong. Maybe what goes wrong is they get complacent. The first few times, they keep everything meticulously clean, but then they start to relax, maybe figuring that they don't have to go crazy. In fact, they do. I couldn't hope to match Darren's knowledge or Lake of Bays' technology, but I could at least try to emulate their cleanliness.

FAT LOT OF good it would do me.

"I'm sure there's more," I said to Catharine. I held a beautifully formed barley head in my hand. Lovely fat kernels ran in two opposite rows up the sides of the stalk, some capped with the barley's trademark beards, those long, thin whisker-like shoots that sprout from the tops of the kernels. If a film producer called up a casting agent and said I want a barley stalk for a commercial I'm making, this is what they would send over.

I'd picked this stalk to show to Catharine, who was involved in some mysterious farm-related business in the erstwhile chicken coop. When we got back to the farm from my week at Lake of Bays, I knew things were bad in the barley field, and I was spending my first morning back working my way through the patch, all dry earth and brown, crispy, stunted strands, many speckled with what I took to be mold. But when I found this handsome stalk I took it as a sign—something had survived. Maybe if we really scoured the field, we could put together enough barley to make some beer—even just one batch. Catharine is far more conscientious than I am, so I prayed that if she came back up the hill with me she'd be able to turn up more of the right stuff, something resembling mature, usable barley. She agreed to have a look, and I wasn't disappointed. Carefully parting the dry stalks with her hands, turning over the heads with her fingers, she found... another stalk.

"That" she said, pointing to the barley head in my hand, "is half your crop. And this"—she pointed to the stalk she'd found—"is the other half."

Conversely, the hops were doing great.

IT'S ALL ABOUT THE HOSES

DARREN'S RED ALE, "POPOCATEPETL"

As with most brewers, Darren Smith of Lake of Bays Brewing treats the recipe for his rousse, now known as Spark House, as a closely guarded secret. Darren was willing, however, to share this recipe for a reddish ale named after the massive active volcano visible from Mexico City (perhaps for its explosive flavor). This was one of the thirteen "pilot" brews that led to the final recipe for Spark House.

An all-grain recipe, Popocatepetl features no fewer than five different types of malt. Canadian two row makes up the bulk of it and provides the enzymes that will do the actual converting. Carafoam is a caramelized malt that gives the beer its color and a malty sweet flavor. Crystal malt also adds to the sweetness of the final beer. Acidulated malt contains a small amount of lactic acid. Black patent malt, as you might guess, is a roasted malt that gives a highly roasted flavor, but also fruity hints of currants, blackberries or even sultanas. This is one complex grain bill. The crystal malt in the recipe is 10-L, a reference to the Lovibond scale. Developed by Joseph William Lovibond, this system measures the color of beer by breaking it into standard shades. A light golden lager might be a 2 or a 3, a pale ale anywhere from 10 to 13, and so on to the darkest stouts as high as 70 on the scale. As seems to be the case with every known form of beer measurement, the Lovibond scale was superseded by the color units in the EBC (European Brewery Convention) system, though as with every other form of beer measurement, both systems are in use. Amarillo hops are a newish strain from the American West Coast, similar in some ways to Cascade and very popular with home brewers. They are trademarked and their precise ancestry kept secret.

These measurements are for a ten-gallon reddish pale ale, but it would be simple to halve the recipe.

GRAIN BILL

12 lbs Canadian two row

2 lbs Carafoam

3 lbs Crystal 10-L

1 lbs Acidulated malt

4 oz Black patent malt

(Total 18 lbs 4 oz)

HOPS BILL

1 oz Centennial (60 minutes)

1 oz Amarillo (30 minutes)

2 oz Saaz (15 minutes)

"POPOCATEPETL"

YEAST

California Common Ale Yeast

OG: 1.051

FG: 1.012

Method: Heat 7 U.S. gallons of water to 167 degrees Fahrenheit. Add grain and steep for 1 hour. Target temperature is 149 degrees Fahrenheit. Sparge grains at 172 degrees Fahrenheit, bringing volume up to 11 gallons. Boil for 60 minutes, adding hops as indicated. Remove from heat. Bring the total volume to 10 gallons. Strain. Cool to 170 degrees Fahrenheit and pitch yeast. Rack to secondary fermenter when gravity is stable. Prime, bottle and age at room temperature for at least 2 weeks before chilling.

Five

SOMETIMES, BREWING IS NOT PRETTY

IT SEEMED TO me I had three choices.

One. Give up. I could manage pretty much without everything else but not without my barley. So I should just call it quits.

Two. Lie. Who needs to know? I could go on making beer using malt I'd bought, and no one would be any the wiser. When I got down to writing about it, I'd make sure to toss in the odd line about "rippling waves of ripening barley," their "heads bent as if in supplication to Gambrinus, the legendary patron saint of beer" and lots of other good atmospheric stuff. That would cover it. I mean, it's all about expectations, and as long as I satisfied people's expectations, everything would be fine. Except that liars always seem to get caught—look at that whiz kid at the *New Yorker* or the guy who made up a story about that Apple factory in China for National Public Radio. I might be safe for a few months, maybe even a year, but somehow, some way, the truth would come out. Maybe one of the farm members would rat me out as part of one of the complex vendettas that occasionally seep into the place. Or an envious clerk at the home brew supply place would expose me.

However it happened, I'd have to issue a groveling apology. I could see it—the snapping cameras, Catharine standing off to one side, accompanied perhaps by some blond children, if we could rent them, smiling bravely and watching while I debased myself, tearfully citing the "hurt I caused my family... and beer writers everywhere" and then announcing I was "embarking on a journey of personal healing." True, I could probably recoup something afterward by writing a self-justifying memoir, but frankly? More trouble than it was worth.

There was a third option. I could try to find someone near our farm who had barley and would let me harvest some of it. Two row if I could get it, but any kind of barley if it came to that. The pioneers hadn't been picky, and I shouldn't be either. It wouldn't be mine, but it would be local, dammit. And when you thought about it, I'd still have done everything myself: planted barley, cultivated it and then harvested it—just not the same barley. It was worth a shot.

I WAS THINKING these thoughts lying, once again, flat on my back on my office floor. Back at the farm on the weekend, after I had seen that my crop was a failure, I had basically sunk to my knees in the parched field and brandished a fist at the heavens.

Then I'd started pulling purple loosestrife out from around the pond. Sort of agrarian grief therapy, I guess. Loosestrife is a highly invasive nonnative plant that sends out a tough net of roots, and it is hell to dig up—you need to pry up the whole mat of roots. I'd been working with a fork on a particularly large and particularly resistant clump and was pulling on the stalks when I felt a constriction in the small of my back. I stopped pulling, but my back felt tight and stayed that way for the rest of the week. Then on Thursday morning, while I was getting ready to use a car jack to pop the lock on Catharine's bicycle (a useful trick when the key snaps off in the lock), a bolt of lightning shot up my back just as I was leaning forward. By that afternoon, I could barely walk. We had planned a special trip to a great beer supply place in Brampton to pick up supplies for my next brew. I was a sight, navigating the store aisles bent ninety degrees at the waist and trying to ask the clerk questions by twisting my head to one side and then cocking it upward to meet his eye, just like Charles Laughton in *The Hunchback of Notre Dame*. By Friday morning, I could make it maybe ten feet before I had to sit down. Just as well I didn't have any barley, because I sure wouldn't have been able to harvest it.

But how would I find barley? I wasn't quite sure, but the first person I could think to ask was Peter Johnson, my agriculture ministry expert. Peter had no idea. He didn't know eastern Ontario. Instead he put me in touch with Scott Banks, the guy who covered our part of the province. Not for the first time did I appreciate that the telephone was a farmer's most useful tool.

Scott gave me the names of a couple of seed suppliers and the number for a grain elevator in my area. There was a chance, just a chance, that these people might know a farmer out there who had the barley I needed. The people at the elevator thought there was a local farmer who might still have two row in his fields. He didn't. But when we talked on the phone, he agreed to sell me eighty pounds of two row for a princely ten bucks. He was located a haul from the farm, two hours at least, but if I couldn't come up with anything else, his barley would save me. Then I called a seed company farther up the valley. I got a name: Mike Wilson. He farmed over on the Quebec side of the Ottawa River, not far from us. At least in distance.

DOBERMAN OR MASTIFF? Or maybe a mixture of both? I couldn't really say. But it was dark and big and the cinder block connected to the long chain clipped onto its collar suggested that this was a dog that meant business. Ditto the two slightly smaller dogs behind it. I took them to be its—her—pups. Millie barked, emboldened perhaps by the fact that we were safely inside Mike Wilson's Ford F-150.

He had taken me to see his barley in a field near his house, then decided he wanted to talk to the tenant he had living in the farmhouse there. While they chatted in the driveway, Millie and I sat in the truck. I, at least, was careful not to make eye contact with what seemed like three canine refugees from a particularly nasty German folktale.

"Does she breed dogs?" I asked Mike as we headed back to his house.

"Not intentionally," he said.

When I'd called Mike the previous Friday and explained myself, he had told me that he was close to cutting his barley, but he promised that if I couldn't get there before then, he would leave me some to do myself. Between my sciatica and the fact that the morning I had originally planned to drive to western Quebec, I had awoken to find the street in Toronto dug up and our car completely boxed in by emergency vehicles (an ancient brick-lined sewer had collapsed), it had taken me a week to finally meet up with him.

It's odd. I've been going to the Ottawa Valley for thirty-two years, and Catharine's been going for even longer, but in all that time, we had never crossed the Ottawa River to the Quebec side. And the bridge was maybe a half-hour drive from our farm. It just never entered into our minds. Heading for Mike's, I learned that we weren't alone in this attitude. Taking the road north from Renfrew, I missed my turn. I'd assumed there would be a sign saying how far to Shawville, the biggest town on the Quebec side, or even announcing something simple like "Bridge" or "Quebec." No. Apparently the Ontario government doesn't regard the existence of another large province nearby as worthy of comment.

I'd have been willing to chalk it up to Canada's two solitudes, except as I discovered when I came off the bridge into Quebec, actually a two-lane road running along the curving top of a hydro dam that straddled the Ottawa River, I didn't seem to have left Ontario. Say "rural Quebec" and what I think of are gray stone houses and towns dominated by hulking *églises,* each featuring a steeple coated with that matte aluminum paint that seems to be the exclusive property of the Roman Catholic Diocese of Quebec. Instead, what I saw were red brick farmhouses and small Protestant churches. Valley culture, I realized, didn't respect the provincial boundary and, up here it seemed, had developed independently of it. With one major difference, though: the shabby town I was passing through and the potholed road I was driving on to reach Mike Wilson's house in Starks Corners reminded me of the Ontario side thirty years ago. Sometimes when Catharine is trying to explain the valley's relative isolation and ruggedness to people who have never been there, she will use a helpful phrase she picked up from an economist who studied the area: "The east is the north of the south." Northern Ontario, which makes up 90 percent of the province's land mass, is a vast, thinly inhabited expanse of rocks, lakes and muskeg. The south, with the exception of eastern Ontario, is nicely rolling hills, prosperous farming towns and big cities. Folks from the south may not know eastern Ontario, but they do (or think they do, thanks to the obligatory Group of Seven painting of a bent tree that's reproduced in every Ontario school) know the north, and that gives them something they can understand.

Well, by that measure, western Quebec is like the north of the east. When I pulled into Mike's steep, sloping driveway, he was underneath his daughter's Impala changing the oil. He'd been expecting me. Mike was in his fifties, a ruddy-faced man with a couple of days' growth of beard. I noticed that he was smoking Putter's, the knock-off version of Player's ostensibly sold only on First Nations reserves. His house was a gray brick product of the seventies, across the road from a very old United Church. Next door was an old one-room schoolhouse. The Roman blinds in the school's windows made me wonder if gentrification might finally be reaching western Quebec.

To survive as a farmer anywhere in this part of the valley, actually anywhere in the valley, come to that, you need to be flexible and diversified. Mike had sheep. He had draft horses and competed in plowing matches. He owned two separate farms, the one where he lived and the one farther down the road leading to Ontario where he had taken me to see the barley. He used to work in the bush in the winter. He worked as the mechanic at a nearby organic farm.

And now he was branching out into running his own microbrewery. His goal was similar to mine, if even more ambitious: create a beer that was entirely—water, grain and hops—local. And to that end, he had several dozen acres of two-row barley under cultivation. Another nearby farmer, Tim Wickens, could provide the hops.

The provincial government was only too happy to help him. Known as the Pontiac, this part of Quebec had lost its lumber mill and its mine in recent years. The biggest surviving local employer was the organic farm that Mike worked for, which employed around twenty people, ten locals and the rest migrant workers from Mexico and Jamaica.

Mike hoped to set up his brewery in a disused clapboard cheese factory that stood not far from his house. "Providing I cross all my *t*'s and dot all my *i*'s," he told me, "the government will pay up to 60 percent of my costs." First, he'd like to wangle a heritage grant. He told me he had pushed the building around a bit with a grader to straighten it up, but to my eyes it still seemed to list a trifle.

Mike drove us back to his place, and then Millie and I got into our Honda Fit and headed back to the barley patch. We had us some harvesting to do. I took my blue tarpaulin out of the back of the Fit and draped it over the single strand of barbed wire topping the page wire fence surrounding Mike's barley field. Then I dropped Millie over. I tossed my tarpaulin over, grabbed my sickle from the car, slipped it through the page wire, and then clambered over, taking care to keep that lone rusty strand of barbed wire well away from my more tender bits. I thought of Mike's line when we'd come by earlier: "I'll bet you don't climb too many fences in Toronto."

Looking around, I saw what I should have seen at our farm: golden barley, about eighteen inches high, the heads drooping and the seed kernels large. Just the way everyone described it.

Millie parked herself in the weeds. I spread out the tarpaulin on a bare patch of ground. I'd found my late father-in-law's sickle when we were cleaning out the basement of our house getting ready to sell. It was an exquisitely rusty tool, except for the glint of the curved edge that I had sharpened using a grinding wheel. Because it was so sharp, I had to be careful with it, and so it was the last thing I had packed in the car late the night before. Still doubled over with sciatica, with a discernible limp, I had shuffled across our dark urban street with it dangling loosely in one hand, its clean edge glinting in the streetlight's glow. Someone walking up the street caught sight of me, did a double take and then turned on his heel quickly.

My back was still bothering me, but sickling or scything, or whatever it was, turned out to be one hell of a lot easier than I had expected. Sickles have been around a very long time, and over the millennia, they have evolved to be really ergonomically comfortable. Once I was bent over and cutting, it was easy going. I'd grab a big handful of barley, fairly far down the stems, squeeze them together tight, and then slash with the sickle, always making sure that I slashed away from my leg. It wouldn't have taken my foot off or anything, but I had no desire to drive to the nearest emergency room (about twenty kilometers distant over a bad road by my estimation) with blood filling my running shoe.

I cut then tossed each handful of barley onto my tarpaulin. It was filling quite quickly, but the bulk wasn't what I would term the business part of the barley—the seed kernels or barleycorn that I hoped to turn into malt. It was mostly just stems, leaves and assorted chaff—as I thought that word to myself, I realized that this was the first time in my life I had ever used it to refer to what it actually meant. Given how much extraneous trash seemed to be filling my tarpaulin, maybe, I thought, it would be best if I just snapped the ears off the barley. Not so much harvesting it, really, as picking it, like grapes. Putting aside my sickle, I started grabbing the barley heads and snapping them off. It was cleaner, yes, but also much, much slower. I'd need the better part of a week to harvest enough barley for a barrel of beer.

I slashed away for the better part of an hour and a half. Cars rolled by a few feet away, and near four o'clock, the school bus pulled up and a couple of kids got out. In the end, I had cleared a twenty-by-thirty-foot patch. I wouldn't really know how much usable grain I had until I threshed it or winnowed it— or whatever the hell I was supposed to do with it. With my harvest wrapped in the blue tarpaulin in the back of the car, we headed back to Ontario.

I FIGURED WHEN I decided to try brewing beer from scratch that I'd face plenty of challenges. Farming challenges. Brewing challenges. Drinking challenges. I never expected ethical challenges. What to do when my barley crop failed had been one. Now I faced another.

Everything I had read about barley had been false. No problem with weeds; just stick it in the ground and it comes on up. Oh, and it doesn't need to be watered. Lies, lies, lies. Happily, though, most of what I read about hops was also a lie. Notably, don't expect much from your hop plants the first year, I'd read—after I'd got embroiled in making beer.

But the hops had done fine. My kick-ass Nugget, the one that came up first and fastest, had a ton of cones drooping on it. The others had come through, too, but the Nugget alone looked to have given me enough for a few brews. I inspected the yield more closely when I got back from Quebec. The cones were turning a little brown along the edges. It might have been nice to get them a few days earlier, but it wasn't the end of the world. I filled several ziplock sandwich bags with them and took them with me when we headed back to Kingston.

Once you pick hops, you need to dry them fairly quickly; otherwise, the oils that give them their oomph start to break down. You have to rig a system so that the air can circulate around them freely and they're out of direct light. I had some nylon screen, but I really needed a frame for it. Okay, I'm aware at this point that what I am going to say sounds like self-justification, but bear with me. I didn't have the right wood around the house, and I couldn't spare the time to go to a lumberyard in Kingston the next morning before heading back to Toronto. Fortunately, it was Monday night, garbage night. I went out hunting. You never know what people are going to toss out.

Just up the street, in front of a semidetached cream-colored brick house, I found just the thing. A three-by-three-foot frame made of two-by-fours with a piece of plywood the same size screwed to it. I flipped it over. Tack some screen to the two-by-fours on this side, and it would make a great rack for drying hops.

As anyone who has ever sifted through their neighbor's garbage knows, there are established rules of thumb about taking objects from in front of people's houses. If someone has put, say, a piece of furniture right down by the street, you can have it. This is particularly true on garbage day. But it has to be right down on the street. If you take a deck chair off someone's porch, that's stealing. My newly discovered hop-drying rack—so perfect for my pressing need—was near the street, but leaning against the metal railing of the front steps. A gray area.

Worse, I knew this house—the owners were a young doctor and her chef husband. In fact, I'd met them at a Christmas party given by their next-door neighbor. Nice people. He was a vibrant man, possessor of a grand smile and an enormous gnarled ginger beard. Lanky and chestnut-haired, she reminded me of my own daughter.

It was late evening now. Too late to ask them if it was all right to take it—all the lights were off. And I had to get going in the morning.

Take it! said the evil little Ian the brewer on my left shoulder. *They want you to take it. No, no,* said the angelic Ian the brewer on the opposite shoulder. *It's not at the curb.*

I paced up and down. I looked around. Quickly, I hefted the stand up and started walking fast toward our house.

SOMETIMES, BREWING IS not pretty. Particularly when it requires period clothing.

"Will you want a tie?" The head of the wardrobe department at Black Creek Pioneer Village and I were putting together my costume for my first day of work.

I'd made this trek to the outer edge of Toronto because I wanted to gain some insight into historical brewing methods. I wasn't necessarily setting out to brew historic beer, but what I was doing did have a lot in common with brewing 150 years ago—around the time the first settlers took possession of the land on which the farm now stood. So it seemed like a good idea to understand how beer was made back in day, so to speak, using fairly simple ingredients and rudimentary equipment. I'd read as many old brewing tracts as I could get my hands on. (This included one volume so old that the *s*'s all looked like *f*'s. The constant references to "yeaft"—or "yeft," as that word hadn't yet gained its "a"—took a while to get used to.)

Then I learned about the Black Creek Brewery. Aha! A way to do more than just read about old brewing methods. The local conservation authority runs a historic theme park named Black Creek Pioneer Village in Toronto's northwest suburbs. I think it's one of those places that are essentially based on colonial Williamsburg, and we've all been to them. There's a collection of period buildings, often rescued from urban inundation, or even literal flooding, all given over to various period endeavors: blacksmithing, tin stamping and rock candy manufacturing, carried out by people in period dress. A couple of years earlier, Black Creek had opened a pioneer brewery, said to be the only one of its kind operating in North America.

I'd approached Black Creek months ago about working in the brewery. But my desire to learn about nineteenth-century brewing had been delayed for a thoroughly twenty-first-century reason—the question of legal liability in case I inadvertently tumbled into a brewing kettle or was crushed by a hogshead of ale. I can only imagine the historic villages in the future that will portray twenty-first-century life: kids will don helmets to watch people dressed in authentic costumes stitch warning labels onto beach towels. And, of course, the highlight of the trip will be a visit to the litigator.

The legalities finally ironed out, the head of wardrobe and I were in a large room filled with period dresses, coats, top hats and bonnets in the basement of the modern visitors' center. I'd already picked out a pair of brown homespun trousers with suspenders, a waistcoat and a blue-and-brown check shirt. I would have preferred an apron or a leather jerkin, but they weren't on offer. So a scarf tied insouciantly around my neck seemed like a good detail. I wanted to fit in. On Catharine's insistence, I had not trimmed my beard or hair for several weeks. This, she assured me, would make me look more authentic; I told myself it made me look like the Unabomber. But that was too flattering. When I checked my outfit in the mirror, I had that same sheepish, self-conscious expression you see on a dog's face when you dress it up in a shirt and tie. I was the human version of a William Wegman photo.

Black Creek's brewery is located in the basement of an old inn called the Half Way House that had once stood on Kingston Road in Toronto's east end. Housing the brewery in the former tavern, now relocated to the other side of the city, was an authentic touch. In the earlier parts of the nineteenth century, in rural areas particularly, a tavern or inn would have made its own beer—such brewers as there were, in our sense of the word, wouldn't have shipped their product much more than a few miles beyond the towns where they were located. Historically, however, a tavern's brewing operation wouldn't have been in a cellar. They might have stored beer there but not brewed it—the more likely spot would have been in a room just behind the bar. In this case, space constraints had trumped authenticity.

I'd enjoyed my time at Lake of Bays, though its relevance to my brewing endeavors seemed a bit tenuous. The scale and degree of technical sophistication were a long way from anything I could replicate. I felt that the three days I planned to spend at Black Creek would be considerably more useful. Whatever tips on the ingredients and techniques of 150 years ago I could take away with me by working with Black Creek's brewmaster, Ed Koren, would be helpful when it came to brewing my perfect keg.

For home brewers, Ed's job is a dream come true. A prizewinning amateur beer maker and a butcher by training, Ed had been a manager in the meat department at a Sam's Club when he was suddenly laid off in 2008. He'd been out of work all of a week when he received a chance e-mail from a friend telling him about Black Creek's new brewery. He applied and was originally taken on to do just one day a week. In 2009, he became the full-time brewmaster. Ed told me that years ago, when he was stationed with the Canadian army in Germany, he had loved dropping in on little inns that brewed their own beer, never imagining that one day he would be doing the same thing.

Tall, goateed and balding—and a damned sight more convincing in his nineteenth-century clothes than I could ever hope to be—Ed was already heating the water for mashing in on the low brick stove when I pulled open the door to the brick-walled brewery room. Ed works his way through a number of historic beer styles each week, and this first morning, he told me, we were going to be brewing brown ale. I mentally scanned the list that Ian Bowering had given me. Brown ale hadn't appeared, but I would later learn from Ed that brown ale and dark ale had been one and the same in the nineteenth century, and were sometimes referred to simply as ale. In the mid-nineteenth century, especially in rural areas, malting would have been done over direct heat, and as a result, the barley would have been baked quite brown. In fact, one of the varieties of malt Ed used is roasted a rich brown over a hardwood fire, and I could smell smokiness in it. (It is a bit of a departure from historical authenticity, but Ed uses commercially produced modern malt and hops in his brewing.) Call it brown, call it dark, call it plain old ale, the resulting beer was a very dark brown. Compared with pale ales, it was only lightly hopped and hence nowhere near as bitter.

I worked with Ed for three days, brewing pale ale the next day and stout on a Sunday, but as had been the case at Lake of Bays, the routine didn't differ from beer to beer.

How damned simple it was. The rig Ed used was based on period photographs and descriptions of nineteenth-century breweries, and it used just two vessels: a mash tun and a kettle. These cost $14,000 to custom-make today and were arc-welded, not a technique the pioneers would have gone in for.

First, we'd dump a pile of milled grain into the mash tun, which resembled an enormous wooden washtub with a tap stuck in the bottom. Next to go in was the hot water. To heat it, Ed used a kettle, an equally enormous copper pot with a conical lid that sat atop a low brick oven. Historically, this would have been heated by wood; Ed's stove uses gas. We poured buckets of the hot water over the grain and then I got to mash it in, using a large wooden paddle to turn and turn the grain so that it got uniformly wet. Brewers were using thermometers by the mid-nineteenth century, but Ed knows the process so well that during the three days I was with him, I don't think I ever saw him pick one up.

When we'd finished mashing in, we drained the tun and poured the wort back into the now empty kettle. Interestingly, Ed didn't sparge—that is, strain water through the used grains to eke out a little more sugar. That's quite authentic. Old-time brewers didn't sparge either—as a result, the first pour-through was only about 75 percent effective—but reused their mash to make what was called "small" or "table" beer. These were low-alcohol brews that everyone, including children, drank rather than take their chances with bad water.

After the wort had boiled for a good hour, we poured it through cheesecloth into a cooling vessel—really just a large flat tray. The one at Black Creek had copper pipes running through it that carried cold water and chilled the beer more quickly. I was surprised by this, but Ed told me later these cooling coils were used in the olden days, in those cases where the brewer had access to a source of cool running water nearby, say a stream or brook. The whole setup was gravity fed—from the cooling vessel, the beer ran down a skinny rack located over a spigot turned upward so that the beer poured right into a wooden barrel. When it finished fermenting, Ed would turn the spigot in this first barrel and the beer would dribble into a second one sitting directly under it. I wanted to use a real wooden barrel for my beer, so I was intrigued to see Ed's. I learned from him, though, that they weren't authentic—they were actually whiskey barrels. Barrel, shmarrel, I thought, aren't they all the same? No, I learned—these barrels hold liquid all right, but the carbon dioxide produced by fermentation seeps out between the seams. Black Creek has not been able to find actual beer barrels, which are much thicker walled and, I would imagine, even more tightly seamed. Finishing up, Ed put a piece of cheesecloth over the open bung in the top of the first barrel, which we would peel back to toss in the yeast.

As Ed explained it, the function of the brewery is primarily to provide an educational experience and only secondarily to make beer. Black Creek runs brewery tours that start off exploring an old mill where the grain for brewing would traditionally have been ground and end up watching Ed at work. Or, for these three days, Ed and his slightly addle-brained helper. The whole time I was there, people were constantly coming into the brewery and asking him questions. People even asked me questions. Mostly about things I didn't know. I answered them anyway.

The highlight of the tour is a sample of whatever Ed is brewing, which I imagine is what draws a lot of people in the first place. Ed, or one of the tour guides, proposes a toast to the Queen (who, back then, would have been Victoria), and then it's bottoms up. It was interesting to note the number of people who really didn't like what they were offered—the appeal of flattish, warmish, brownish beer is lost on many who've cut their beer-drinking teeth on ice-cold Coors and Labatt Blue. Not everyone, mind you, but many. Although as Ed pointed out, the Victorians weren't as spoiled—they couldn't be, when the alternative was water that could make you sick.

I left Black Creek with a growler of old-fashioned beer, a shopping bag full of hops I picked in their garden (their gardener had planted them without telling anyone what variety they were and then quit) and a deep admiration for Ed. His ability to brew using primitive equipment was impressive. Yes, fancy equipment is nice, but care and knowledge will take you a long way. If he could make good beer using two pots and a few barrels, I could do the same. Earlier, I had thought I would do a mild ale for my perfect brew. But now, after working with Ed, I had the beer I thought I should be making: brown ale. I wasn't sure whether our pioneers, people working land like mine, had drunk mild. It was a good bet, though, that they had drunk brown. If politics is the art of the possible, sometimes historic brewing is the art of the probable.

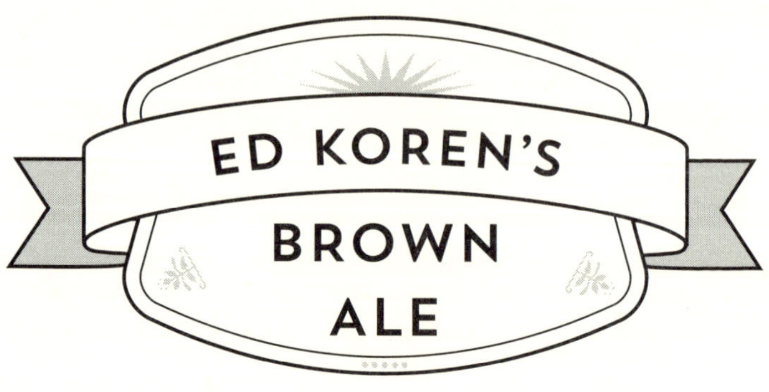

Ed Koren's Brown Ale

ED KOREN TAKES pains to point out that although his recipe is for creating a historic brown ale, it is not itself a historically accurate recipe. Pioneer brown ales would have been made with malt roasted directly over a smoky fire to a dark, almost scorched color. You might not have encountered it in a pioneer-era tavern, but by the late eighteenth century, maltsters had perfected ways of kilning malt with indirect heat. The resulting malt was paler and toasty-looking and contained far more convertible starches. It ushered in the era of beers that were lighter in color and flavor, and higher in alcohol.

Where authenticity comes into this beer is mainly in Ed's brewing techniques. To give it a more authentic taste, he uses modern malt that has actually been smoked. That and the other materials may be modern, but the way he brews is pure nineteenth century—which is similar to the way that many amateur brewers make beer at home today. Assuming your brewhouse efficiency is 75 percent, this single-infusion mash recipe should produce a dark brown/ mahogany-colored beer with a nice caramel-sweet finish.

GRAIN BILL

7.9 lb Marris Otter

1 lb Brown malt

13.2 oz English crystal 77-L

4.4 oz Flaked wheat

4.4 oz Chocolate malt 350-L

(Total 10 lbs 4.4 oz)

HOPS BILL

1 oz Fuggles (4.75% AA) (60 minutes)

1 oz Kent Goldings (5% AA) (20 minutes)

1 oz Kent Goldings (5% AA) (flameout)

Whirlfloc/ Irish moss (last 10 minutes of the boil [optional])

YEAST

Any type of English ale yeast (for example, Safale S-04 [dry])

OG: 1.053

FG: 1.014

Method: Mash grains at 152 degrees Fahrenheit for 60 minutes. Mash out at 168 degrees Fahrenheit for 10 minutes. Sparge and collect about 6.5 U.S. gallons and boil hard for 60 minutes, adding hops and Whirlfloc/Irish moss at appropriate time. Cool the wort to 70 degrees

Fahrenheit and transfer to primary fermenter. Then pitch the yeast and ferment at 70 degrees Fahrenheit for 7 days. Transfer to secondary fermenter and store in as cold an area as you can. Once the beer has cleared up (the colder it is, the faster it will clear up), bottle or keg. For best flavor, age for about 3 weeks.

A CASE OF THE "BUT WAITS"

WHAM! THE DEER'S legs flailed as it rolled up along the hood of the Honda Fit before dropping off into the ditch, where it lay kicking in its apparent death throes.

I felt sick and shaken as we quickly pulled over. I opened the passenger-side door and got out. Catching some movement in the side mirror, I turned and saw the deer bounding off, along the verge and into the woods, seemingly unharmed. Unlike our car, which now had a buckled hood and a shattered left headlight, garnished with a bit of blood and a few delicate pellets of deer shit. We were lucky. Because we'd been coming uphill and rounding a corner, we had dropped our speed. Hitting the animal on a straightaway, going flat out, would have destroyed the car. And maybe us. As it was, the damage to the front of the car complemented the dent in the back of the car. I had backed into a pillar in the underground parking garage at my cousin's place while staying with her during my time at Black Creek Pioneer Village.

When I had harvested my barley at the farrm in Quebec, I had asked Mike to hold some threshed two row for me when he was done with his own harvest. I had my plastic garbage can full of the stuff I'd cut myself, but I figured I would need a fair amount of additional barley to practice on before I made my ultimate keg. His crop was in now, and we had been heading up to our farm, the first leg on our trip to his place, when we hit the deer.

We reached Mike's place in Quebec around eleven the next morning, Sunday, after a night at the farm. The enormous dog that Millie and I had been wary of on our last visit was in the yard as we pulled up behind Mike's truck at his other farm. I was relieved to see that it was still tethered to a cinder block by a long chain, though Mike's tenant told us that in the night the dog had dragged the block far into a nearby field, apparently in hot pursuit of a wolf.

I felt a little better about my own failures when I learned that Mike's harvest had been disappointing, too. (Disappointing is a relative term. He had brought in more than ten tons of two row.) Mike dropped an electrical fence and led me toward the barn behind the brick farmhouse. I sidestepped an enormous chewed bone, a human femur by the look of it. Two-row barley was heaped about three feet high inside a stall against one wall. Mike found me a snow shovel, and I started filling the garbage bags I had brought with the pale brown seed. In the end, I had about forty pounds in each. Enough, I reckoned, for eight or ten brews. Plenty enough to compensate for potential mistakes.

It was largely an impulse, but I figured as long as we were in Quebec, we might want to call on Tim Wickens, the hops farmer Mike had told me about on my earlier trip. Tim was waiting for us just outside an old wooden farmhouse a few minutes away on the road to Shawville. Gray-haired and bespectacled, he possessed a fine valley accent, undiminished by more than two decades away in the big city, in his case working for the board of education in Ottawa. He retired a few years ago and then moved back to this farm, which had been in his family for four generations. (And it was considerably older than that: the original farmer had been granted the land for service at the Battle of Waterloo in 1815.) Not far from his house stood an old lime kiln and the remains of a mill race. This farm was just one of several in the area that he owned. No one around here, it seemed, worked just one patch of land.

We reached Tim's hop field via a small corral holding about a dozen sheep, which mobbed Millie. She escaped by wriggling through a five-bar fence. So much for our long-held belief that her ancestry included border collie, which was based entirely on her occasional display of the crazily intense look that breed often favors.

The hops field consisted of several dozen telephone poles, each about twenty feet tall. The poles were bare now, but in the growing season, the hops would climb thick brown cords running to the top of them. At harvest time, Tim just cut these down and pulled the hops off by hand. He grew about a dozen different varieties.

Tim's field is yet another government-supported attempt at diversifying the local economy, and he is just one of a number of local farmers who are growing hops. (To curry favor with the francophone civil servants sent from Quebec City, Tim said that they made sure to play up their status as oppressed Scots, not haughty English overlords. Relations between this comparatively needy but largely English-speaking district and its faraway French-speaking government seem complex, to put it mildly. That femur I'd seen earlier might well have belonged to some hapless official sent out to guarantee local compliance with the strictures laid down by the Office québécois de la langue française.)

This was Tim's third year farming hops, and his crop had done well. But what happened next was the problem. Some of his and the other farmers' hops had been taken by a collège d'enseignement général et professionnel (CEGEP) with a brewing program, but the farmers didn't really have any other market. I had an idea and as we left I told him I would look into it. In exchange, he promised me hops. The completion of this transaction took on epic proportions but ultimately had a happy ending. I was able to put Tim and his fellow hop growers in touch with Joel Manning of Mill Street Brewery. Mill Street was planning to open an Ottawa brewpub in the coming months and were looking for local suppliers. But the hops I was to get in return proved elusive.

I tried to e-mail Tim, but he had warned me that his dial-up connection was fairly spotty. I began calling instead and leaving messages. Always without an answer.

I grew increasingly worried—to the extent that I began scanning local news online for reports of fires or car accidents. Finally, I did something I hadn't done in years: I sat down, wrote him a letter and thought no more of it. Weeks later, I arrived home one day to find a delivery notice from the post office hung over the doorknob. I couldn't imagine what it was, but I got on my bike and rode off to my local post office. When the clerk, a stocky young fellow who looked pretty much the way I imagined Gimli's son would had that redoubtable Tolkien dwarf ever been blessed with issue, reemerged from the back room, he was carrying a box three feet long by one and half feet wide and two feet tall. Hops from Tim Wickens. I rode home, the box teetering on my handlebars and my knees banging the bottom of it as I pedaled. Between Tim's hops and Mike's barley, I would be able to create numerous practice brews.

AS WELL AS pounds and pounds of practice barley (which we later transferred from garbage bags to burlap sacks that Catharine sewed by hand while we watched old episodes of *Jeeves and Wooster*), I also had the barley that I had hand-harvested in Quebec. Barley in burlap sacks can last for years with no ill effects, but my hand-culled crop was stashed in the henhouse at the farm, wrapped in a tarpaulin and stuffed into a large heavy plastic garbage can. The lid was jammed on firmly so that no mice or chipmunks could get in, but it had been sitting for quite a while and I was nervous about it going bad. When it came to creating my perfect keg, I could not use practice barley. I would brew with only what I had harvested with my own hands. Fine and good, but when I created my final brew, I didn't want to have everyone frenetically doing Saint Vitus' dance thanks to galloping ergot infestation. It had to be stored properly. Storing it meant, of course, preparing it.

It's odd how unaware we are of where a lot of our most popular metaphors or similes come from. Think of "three sheets to the wind" or "take the bit between your teeth," for example. In a world where most of us don't have much to do with sailing ships or riding horses, the original meanings of these turns of phrase aren't always clear. So it's interesting when you encounter a metaphor or a simile in its original context. I soon discovered that working with barley means getting reacquainted with a lot of fairly deeply buried metaphors and similes. You do flail wildly. And you winnow. Just not metaphorically. You really *are* flailing, and you really *are* winnowing. So in these cases, I guess you could call them *literalphors*. And what you are doing isn't *like* separating the wheat from the chaff, you *are* separating grain from the chaff. So that's not a simile, it's a *same-a-le*.

The first step was to separate the barley seed from all the stalks and other crud that I had harvested. From what I could discover in books or online, the best way for the small-scale winnower to do this was to wrap the barley in a tarp and then start whacking. My sources championed a plastic baseball bat as their weapon of choice. I didn't have one, but a lot of sources also mentioned a broom. That I had. After I'd worked it over with that, the experts said, separating the grain from the chaff would be easy. Of course they did.

Using the front porch as our threshing floor, we carefully folded the barley inside a worn blue tarp we'd found in the henhouse. Then I banged it repeatedly with the flat of a broom. It didn't do much. I'd hammer and hammer, and then we'd unfold the tarp to find that I had knocked a lot of kernels loose, but many more steadfastly refused to separate from the stalk. We decided it would be easier instead to work through the barley by hand, picking off the heads manually and squeezing the seeds into a pail. We kept at it for three or four hours, grabbing handful after handful of brown straw, snapping the tops off and tossing the rest aside. It's good work for the middle-aged brain. We needed to finger through handfuls of dry brown barley, find the heads, gather them together, pull them off and cast aside the dross. (At the time I thought that was another literalphor, but it really is a metaphor. The dross is the scum formed by molten metal.) You wouldn't think that snapping the heads off barley was hard work, but it was surprising how well we slept that night.

Next day, with the stalks disposed of, I had a lot of barley still mixed up with little bits of, oh, what I'll call "drossettes"—leftover pieces of gunk smaller than standard dross. The time-honored method for separating the barley (or any grain) from this stuff is to grab handfuls and then toss them in the air. The breeze blows the chaff away and the seeds fall back. I had seen women doing this in some Bollywood video one time, but I have to say that I was dubious—I figured it probably "worked" in the same way a lot of time-honored rustic techniques work, like witching for water. I took the tarpaulin, spread it on the lawn and weighed down the corners with pieces of firewood. Then I dragged my pail over. I grabbed a handful of seeds and fluff and tossed it in the air. Lo and behold, the chaff blew away and the seeds hit the tarpaulin. I tried it again. Same thing. And once more. Before long, I had a collection of barley and the chaff had taken care of itself.

But not much barley. It was humbling, really, how little I had. A couple of hours' work with a sickle got me a garbage can full of barley plants. That and about five additional hours' work had given me maybe five or six pounds of maltable barley. Enough—just, I feared—for my perfect keg. God, what would it have been like if I really had brought in my own much larger barley crop?

THE THINGS YOU learn when you brew beer. Hops and grain absorb water. When cheesecloth gets hot, it burns. Bacteria don't taste good.

Over the fall, Farmer Ian had been getting quite the workout. But life hadn't all been crop failures and hand-harvesting. When I wasn't cursing the heavens for my fate or coveting my neighbors' trash, Brewmaster Ian made his presence felt.

My previous homemade brew, a mix of specialty malts and malt extract, had been fine as far as it went. Easy to do, and easy to get right. But today I was going to make my first all-grain brew, a big, important step on my way to making the perfect keg, a chance to put to use what, if anything, I had learned working at Lake of Bays and Black Creek.

I'd had the idea that because all my ingredients would come from the farm, or very near it, I should do my brewing there as well. Alas, circumstances were not, as they say, propitious. It wasn't just the two plumbers who kept shutting the water on and off all day. Or the electrician and her apprentice punching holes in the kitchen wall beside where I was working. Nor was it the presence of two farm members, one of whom had made a special trip to the farm that day, who were hell-bent on figuring out, once and for all, the source of the sour smell under the kitchen sink. ("*You're smaller, you go in.*") Good work, laudable work, but also work that meant pulling out every last spray bottle of cleaner and box of automatic dishwashing powder and sponge and scouring pad and spreading them across the kitchen floor, a task they carried out in stoic oblivion to my presence in the same room. To this day, I have no idea how or why everyone wound up in the same room at the same time. I just know that at the farm, that's often how things roll.

Of course, it's easy to point a finger at others. And there's a prissy cliché about that: point a finger at someone and there are three pointing right back at you. Too true. If I pointed at the electricians or the plumbers or the farmers and said they were the problem, three fingers, three gnarled fingers with dirty, chipped nails, were aiming right at my chest.

Finger one. Brewing with all grain can be messy—doing a five-gallon, nineteen-liter-ish lot takes about ten pounds of grain. The grain ends up saturated with water, and from my time working with other brewers, I knew you wound up with a mess that resembled nothing so much as demented Weetabix. You can try straining this out with a sieve or a colander once you have finished mashing in, but I thought a much simpler solution would be to load my grain into a cheesecloth bag bound up with string. I'd drop the bag into hot water to start my mashing in and then fish it out at the end.

What I learned was that buying a cheap brewing kettle had been a false economy. When I started mashing in, the (very) full cheesecloth bag rested on the bottom of the pot, which in turn sat on the largest burner on our electric stove. Maybe the same pot on a gas stove would have been all right. With gas I get the feeling that the heat would have played more broadly over the whole bottom of the pot. Conversely, maybe a heavier pot on an electric burner might have been okay. Thicker metal, better dispersed heat. What was not okay was a thin metal pot on an electric burner. When I pulled the bag out, a sizable section of it stayed behind. The charred edges of the hole in the bag told me it had burned onto the bottom of the pot. I poured off the wort into every container I could find and scraped the charred cloth off the bottom of my brew kettle, where it had burned onto the enameled metal in the shape of the rings of the element.

That wasn't my only mistake. Then came...

Finger two. At the end of the boil, when I strained all the saturated hops I'd used out of the brew kettle, a good deal of the wort went with them, leaving me well short of the promised five gallons. At first, I was baffled about where it went. But then I understood. People who follow the instructions—people who read them, actually—know to have a standby pot holding a gallon or more of boiled water to top up their wort.

Finger three. But to be honest, my biggest problem was my decision to brew at the farm rather than at our house in Kingston. My quest for brewing authenticity led me to brew authentically terrible beer.

The day I brewed, I was in an insane hurry. Not just because of the plumbers and electricians but because I had to get going. It was to do with getting the house ready to sell. I could picture all too well Catharine tapping her foot even as she plumped pillows, thinking dark thoughts about her husband mucking about with wort at the far end of the province when there were still endless fluffings on the agenda.

When the brewing was through, I hastily chilled the beer using my cooler, poured it into my large white plastic primary fermenter, slapped the lid on and stuck in the air lock. Then I humped it down to the basement and tucked it in under the cellar stairs, where it sat for the next two weeks. When I transferred it over to the secondary fermenter, it had a faintly banana aroma. And when I bottled it, it didn't taste all that good—but it never does at that stage.

It was when I opened the first bottle a few weeks later, alas, that the true flavor asserted itself. Think Band-Aid. I guess that's another simile, though it doesn't have a "like" in front of it to set it up. But it sure is accurate. The flavor wasn't overwhelmingly Band-Aid, really, like chewing on a couple of them, but more subtle. Just a hint—a *soupçon,* in every sip, if you will.

I was proud of the work that had gone into this brew (my first all-grain batch, my first using liquid yeast and the first where I did an iodine test at home), but having to drink our way through this batch was going to be more chore than pleasure—despite the comment of an artist friend of ours who said she thought Band-Aid beer sounded "really postmodern."

It's too bad you can only point three fingers back at yourself. Because if I'd had a few more, I could have kept on going.

Finger four. Having schlepped the brew back to Kingston, I bottled it in the bathtub. Normally I like to work on the ceramic floor downstairs. But at the time, this area was full of boxes and the pieces of Catharine's disassembled loom, detritus from our final chaotic departure from our old house minutes before the listing went live. Bottling in the bathtub did make it nominally easier to clean up, but because I had to lean over the edge of the tub, I couldn't see clearly how full each bottle was getting. I had a lot of overflow as a result, and this was one of the reasons why I filled fewer bottles than I might have expected: thirty-six rather than forty. But really, how much Band-Aid beer would anyone want?

I WASN'T QUITE sure what had gone wrong with this batch. The most likely explanation? It had sat too long on the yeast. Generally, you leave the beer in the primary fermenter for four or five days, maybe a week, and then transfer it over to a glass carboy. One of the reasons you do this is to get your beer away from the buildup of bacteria and dead yeast that goes with fermentation. With this brew, it was two weeks before I could get back to it and switch it to the secondary fermenter.

So I started working my way through Papazian. You could call Charlie Papazian the king of home brewing. At least in North America. He first published my mainstay, *The Complete Joy of Homebrewing*, back in the early 1980s, and by this point it has gone through four separate editions and countless printings. I would guess it is verging on selling a million copies. Papazian has a favorite catchphrase: "Relax. Don't worry. Have a home brew." It's a phrase that I think helps aspiring home brewers keep things in perspective. Although given my ability to create catastrophes, if I had followed his advice literally, I would have wound up a stumbling, slurring disaster. His little linguistic tic apart, Papazian is probably the best source on how to brew at home—he's logical and exhaustive. And one of the best things is that he sees brewing as open-ended. You can substitute ingredients, you can screw around, subject to certain constraints—and it's all okay.

Until this point, what I had been doing had been fairly straightforward, so I had just dipped into him when I needed a specific piece of advice. But after the case of the vanishing wort and the Band-Aid beer, I thought I had better get a bit more systematic. So I sat down and read him from beginning to end.

ACRID BLUE SMOKE filled the kitchen. Coughing and weeping, I fumbled for the silicone oven mitts, while Catharine lifted the pot off the metal plate straddling two stove burners. I grabbed the smoldering plate, and she tore ahead of me down the stairs to open the front door. I had to hurry—the hot plate was beginning to burn my fingers through the mitts. I thundered outside and tossed it into a snowbank in the laneway where I watched it, sizzling and hissing, sink slowly out of sight.

In theory, having Catharine onside as the official perfect keg brewmistress would make my beer quest a lot easier. In fact, she had been helping me all along whenever I needed an extra pair of hands or some advice. That aside, I had to admit to some mixed feelings when in December she offered to help me more directly with my project. Mixed, in the same way Canada's and Britain's feelings were when the United States finally entered the Second World War. You kidded yourself that, somehow, ultimately, you could have done it on your own, so how dare they show up? But, in general, you were grateful that their resources and ingenuity were at your disposal. Catharine is a great cook and a trained scientist, so I thought she'd bring a measure of know-how and method to my haphazard brewing.

Well, that was the theory.

We had decided to start making smaller batches. It made sense. We needed to make a lot of batches (and, as always, it must be said, drink them—without endangering our lives or our livers). Standard beer recipes yield five U.S.

gallons, about nineteen liters, but we decided to slash this to two gallons, or about eight liters, which in turn worked out to sixteen 500-milliliter bottles. This way, we could do several lots in the next few months.

For our first cobrew, as I thought of it, I had a porter recipe, inspired by Papazian. I say "inspired by" because we didn't have exactly the right ingredients to follow it. We had some crystal malt but not quite enough; the recipe didn't call for it, but we had tons of roasted barley. And we didn't have the exact yeast strain called for, either. However, using a handy-dandy recipe builder that we found on the Brew Your Own website, and then creating a spreadsheet to recalculate amounts, Catharine was able to rejig the recipe for two gallons. So new yeast, new grain, new amount—definitely not the same great recipe.

I wanted to figure out some way of avoiding the problem I had at the farm with the cloth bag burning onto the bottom of the pot. The more we talked about it, the more a large metal plate seemed the way to go. Setting this on the burner, and then putting the pot on top of that, would diffuse the heat. Not only that, a large enough plate could straddle two burners, giving us both greater and more consistent heat.

Finding the plate was easy—when you live four or five scant blocks from a shipyard. Ten minutes rooting in the dumpsters behind the large corrugated metal shed where Metalcraft Marine puts together high-speed fireboats for customers all over the world turned up exactly what we needed: an aluminum plate two feet by about eight inches and probably slightly less than a quarter of an inch thick.

Again, the things you learn from brewing. For example, aluminum smoke is not toxic (at least according to Wikipedia), but it does react chemically with other materials in strange ways. When the smoke had cleared and we had climbed back upstairs to our second-floor kitchen, we saw that the stove's burners were a strange ash color and the black metal rings that surrounded them were badly pitted. Worst of all, the top of the stove was coated in a sticky brown stain that I was still working on removing with Fantastik a month later.

There was another way to avoid the burning problem. I grabbed a smaller but far heavier shiny steel pot from the drawer under the cook top. I filled this with three-quarters of a gallon of well water before throwing it on the burner. We could mash in using this, and then pour it into the bigger pot for the boil.

When you mash in using an all-grain recipe, you end up with a very thick porridge. But even allowing for that, something seemed wrong with the consistency. I added and added grain, but there was no way the three-quarters of a gallon of water could ever possibly absorb all of it. A quick check of our recipe revealed that we had a pound of crystal malt too much. Catharine had properly calculated the amounts by which to reduce the original recipe, but she had then, for some unknown reason—which might explain why she never actually became a scientist, despite that training—weighed out a different amount, and now we had far too much. A quarter of the recipe too much.

Which actually would have worked with our next mistake. Again, there were some issues with dealing with a shrunken recipe. Here was the challenge: we knew that once we had finished pouring additional hot water over it to sparge the grain, we needed to top up the pot with well water to bring it up to two and a half gallons. Over the course of an hour-long boil, this would gradually be reduced to two gallons. So that we would know the right amount, we used a four-cup measuring cup to measure two and a half gallons of water into my big brewing pot. Then we stuck a piece of adhesive tape on the side of the pot at that level. Eleven centimeters equaled two and a half gallons.

After lunch, we began sparging by pouring the contents of the mash tun into our brew kettle through a colander. Because there wasn't quite enough room in the colander for all the grain, we had a second sparge going on the floor with a steamer. I'd alternate. I took heated water, poured it into the perforated colander and let that run through into the kettle. Every now and then, I'd take the pot on the floor and pour the wort I'd collected in it into the big pot on the stove. There was a rhythm to it: First one pot. Pour, lift, turn and dump. Then the one on the floor. Pour lift, turn and dump. Busy with the pot on the stove, I turned to find Millie with her snout buried in the strainer full of spent grain. I shooed her away and kept pouring.

We sparged and sparged, but, once again, something was wrong. When we looked at our tape mark, it was obvious that the wort was barely rising. We knew we were going to have to make up the shortfall with well water, but we were barely halfway to two and half gallons. On an impulse, Catharine grabbed the steel ruler and measured the height of the piece of tape I had put on. It showed not eleven centimeters but twenty-one. I'd arbitrarily added ten centimeters to the depth. We had thought we were just starting out; in fact, we were just about finished.

Then began what I thought of as the "But waits." Catharine thought it would be good to take the original gravity of the wort. This would give us some idea of its ultimate alcohol content and let us monitor its fermentation. But it also required taking the amount of wort we had, estimating its shortfall from the final amount of fluid we would have, and then combining that percentage of water with some wort in a measuring cup, while ("But wait") allowing for the maple syrup we were going to add. Which in turn ("But wait") required switching from imperial to metric (converting before—no, oops—after we had added the water). Then ("But wait") she changed her mind because the only way to do this accurately was to estimate the gravity by volume, not weight. If the final answer had been "a fish" or "Thursday," it wouldn't have made any less sense than the number we came up with: 1.033. 1.033 what?

But for all that, the beer tasted great.

DOG'S TONGUE PORTER

IF YOU DON'T have access to a dog's tongue, don't worry, you can skip this particular ingredient without severely affecting the flavor of the beer. Or try licking the grain yourself.

Numerous stories abound about the origins of porter and why it gained its name. There doesn't seem to be a definitive answer. We do know that porters were among the first industrial beers, brewed in vast vats known as tuns that could hold literally thousands of gallons. (In 1814, one burst at the Meux Brewery in London, tearing out a wall in the brewery, sweeping away houses and claiming eight lives, some through drowning, others through drunkenness. Porter fanciers knelt in the street to drink the rich brown ale as it ran along the gutters.)

This recipe calls for unmalted roasted barley, which was often used in porter because there was a tax on malted barley. It is one of the ingredients that gave porter its distinctive dark color.

GRAIN BILL

3.5 lbs Maris Otter (pale)

8 oz Crystal

10 oz Roasted barley

6 oz Maple syrup

(Total 5 lbs)

HOPS BILL

0.4 oz Fuggles (for boiling)

0.16 oz Goldings (for boiling)

0.16 oz Goldings (for flavor)

0.4 oz Goldings (for aroma)

YEAST

Lallemand Danstar

Nottingham Ale Yeast (recycled)

OG: 1.052

FG: 1.022

Method: Add crushed grains to 0.75 U.S. gallon of water at 168 degrees Fahrenheit. Hold at 150–155 degrees Fahrenheit for 60 minutes. Sparge with about 1.6 gallons of 170 degree Fahrenheit water. Add water to brewpot to make total volume of 2.4 gallons to allow for evaporation. Add maple syrup and first two hops and boil for 75 minutes. Add flavor hops and ⅛ teaspoon Irish moss and boil for 15 minutes more. Remove from heat, add aroma hops and let sit for 2 to 3 minutes. Remove all hops and chill wort. Pitch the yeast when cool. Ferment and bottle.

Seven

YEAST: THE LITTLEST HOUSE PET

IF I WERE honest about the whole growing and brewing process that I had undertaken in the search for my perfect keg, I would have to admit that, allowing for my incompetence and my anxious, sometimes hysterical, personality, most of the obstacles I'd faced—from tainted beer to toxic smoke—hadn't been all that serious. This was true even of my crop failure. It had seemed pretty dire at the time, but it had turned out all right. Better than all right, really, because it sent me on an adventure into an overlooked corner of Quebec. And gave me a hops connection to boot.

That aside, as late fall had given way to winter, I became increasingly preoccupied with the two genuine challenges I faced in brewing my own beer from absolute scratch. One was malting, about which I'll have more to say later. The other was yeast. Whereas malting was a process, and something that we could master (I hoped), yeast was another matter.

Early on in the project, I had sort of shunted yeast to one side. I didn't want to think about it. And as long as we were doing test brews, I didn't really need to. When we brewed, I just went out and bought commercial yeast, usually but not always in powder form, because that was what my local brewing supply store carried. I didn't even need to buy it all that often. After a while, I started reusing my yeast, pouring it out of the primary fermenter into a Ziploc container that I stuck in the fridge.

Once I had settled on brewing brown ale, largely because it seemed historically authentic and straightforward, I started to worry about yeast: what would I need to be true to my "beeroir," as I thought of my corner of the valley, and where would I find it?

THERE'S A LINE you sometimes hear in beer-making circles: brewers make wort; yeast makes beer. You can make a beer without hops, you can make a beer without barley or, indeed, without any form of malted grain. But you cannot make a beer without yeast.

So yeast is essential, but paradoxically, for a very long time, it was also essentially unknown. People have made beer for millennia, but for most of that time, they were entirely unaware of the existence of yeast. In the early sixteenth century, when the Germans created their famed purity law, the *Reinheitsgebot*, which listed the ingredients allowable in beer making (an early example of a nontariff barrier, I suspect), they didn't mention yeast. According to Chris White and Jamil Zainasheff in their book, *Yeast*, people talked about something they referred to as godisgood, a foamy scum that appeared on the surface of fermenting beer that they skimmed off to make more beer; in fact, it was, or contained, yeast. As brewmasters began doing this, they started, entirely unconsciously, the selective breeding of yeast, developing ever-stronger strains. And all without even being aware of what yeast was.

Because yeast was so little understood, however, beer making was a fraught enterprise. You might brew several successful batches of beer in a row, and then suddenly end up making bad beer, as your yeast mutated or the open vats used for brewing in early times got infected with unpredictable wild yeasts. (A wild yeast can generally be defined as any unwanted yeast.) As early as 1680, the Dutch scientist Anton van Leeuwenhoek, known as the father of microbiology, observed yeast close-up using a primitive microscope, but he didn't realize that it was a living entity. He thought it was a side effect of brewing. It wasn't until the nineteenth century that Louis Pasteur was able to prove finally that yeast was a living thing—a member of the fungus family, in fact—and that it was the secret to fermentation.

According to White and Zainasheff, there are five hundred known separate species of yeast, and each species boasts thousands and thousands of strains. Yeasts are literally everywhere—on fruit, on vegetables and on us. They float through the air. In fact, the first beers came about because yeast just happened to get into a vessel filled with soaking barley and got to work.

The yeast that we have "domesticated," if you will, is named *Saccharomyces,* which means "sugar fungus." (I believe this is a bit of a misnomer, because whatever the strain, whatever the species, all yeasts survive the same way: by consuming sugars.) Yeasts produce alcohol and carbon dioxide as by-products of this consumption, or, as one wise guy put it, they "piss alcohol and fart carbon dioxide." In beer making, the two dominant strains of *Saccharomyces* are *S. cerevisiae* and *S. pastorianus. S. cerevisiae* (as in *cerveza,* probably the most universally understood Spanish word) is ale yeast. *S. pastorianus* produces lager, as its previous scientific name, *S. carlsbergensis* (as in Carlsberg Breweries), suggests. As well as determining, very broadly, what sort of beer we get (ale or lager), yeasts influence the flavor of beer in other ways. They produce esters, volatile combinations of acids and alcohol that create distinctive tastes and aromas in beer—anything from banana to (ugh) industrial cleaning solvent. Or, of course, Band-Aid. (By this point I had stoically drunk my way through almost all the Band-Aid beer. It had not aged well.)

Yeasts reproduce by "budding" other yeast cells. They can also reproduce sexually—a process commonly called "shmooing," probably derived from a long-ago creature in the Li'l Abner comic strip that split into two new shmoos when kicked. *S. pastorianus* was the offspring of *S. cerevisiae* and a wild yeast from Patagonia named

S. eubayanus that made its way from the New World to the Old in the late fifteenth century—hitching a ride on a sailing ship, no doubt, as the age of exploration began.

This isn't all there is to say about yeast. Not at all. Books can, and have, been written about it. I recommend that one by White and Zainasheff for any home brewer who wants to get really, *really* serious about yeast. My challenge, if I wanted to make what I told myself was an authentic brown ale, was to figure out what sort of yeast people in pioneer days had used—especially when they weren't really aware yet that yeast existed.

I hoped that beer historian Ian Bowering, who had originally provided me with my list of popular historic Upper Canadian beers, would once again come to my rescue. I shot off an e-mail: "Where did early brewers get their yeast, or godisgood, or whatever they called it?" Ian replied promptly: "From bakers." It was not yeast as such but starter, a mixture of flour, water and yeast that they always kept going. Whenever they needed to bake, they would just hive some off and toss it into their recipe. What he said made sense. Except, of course, when I tried to answer the next obvious question: Where did the bakers get it?

From brewers, it turned out. Circular, but again, it made sense. A great batch of yeast would have been shared around. And in the old days, brewers didn't make beer in the summer. For one thing, the yeast started mutating in warmer weather, doing unpredictable things to the beer. But before refrigeration, they didn't really have any good ways to preserve their yeast, so, and this is a little conjectural on my part, they handed it over to bakers, who kept on baking bread. In the fall, they would get some starter back from the baker and start brewing again. It's like they had joint custody of the yeast. (I can imagine it. Baker: "Now, Yeast, I want you to know that I love you very, very much but it's time for you to go to stay with the brewer." Yeast: "I won't go. I won't! *I won't!*") It's possible that the yeasts being used in rough and ready country breweries in my part of the world in the nineteenth century had been recycled this way for decades. Using yeast from a baker would be a nice authentic touch—though that yeast itself might not be terribly authentic.

The other idea would be to get a yeast from one of the big commercial companies, such as Wyeast or White Labs (which is run by Chris White himself, coauthor of the definitive yeast tome). Both firms offered a lot of what I would call historically *plausible* yeasts—ale yeasts from all over England that dated back two centuries or even more. I would definitely get something that worked. But the more I thought about it, the more this seemed like kind of a cheat. No, not a cheat, a shortcut. We were using our own hops, our own water and (almost) our own barley, which when we finished with it, would be our very own malt. Maybe we should try for our own yeast.

There are yeasts that live on barley, but I learned in an e-mail from Ronald Subden at the University of Guelph agricultural faculty that they were not the way to go. Subden, a retired professor of agriculture and an expert on yeast, told me that they simply were not strong enough for the job.

We had something else. Two years before, in the summer of 2010, we made cider at our farm. Read a modern book on how to do this and the first thing it will tell you is to wash your apples to get rid of any wild yeasts. Then you use a champagne yeast to ferment the cider instead. This isn't stupid. It is very hard to guarantee what you are going to get with wild yeast. We, however, had ignored this advice, with fantastic results. Perhaps it was just a particularly good year, but the yeast that was on the apples fermented like crazy, bubbling up frantically through the air lock on the carboy, and produced great-tasting, clear cider. As in beer making, when the initial fermentation was done, there was a quantity of light brown goo, called lees, left in the bottom of the carboy. Catharine saved some of the lees, nurtured them into sourdough starter and plunked them into a Ziploc container that she put in the fridge. We had used it every week, at least, since to make sourdough bread, pizza crust and focaccia. But what was interesting was that none of these was terribly sour.

This starter is well traveled. It has ranged from Kingston to our farm and back several times, and part of the starter even made a jaunt to Toronto to some old neighbors who wanted to begin sourdough bread baking. We take it pretty much anywhere we go, in its own little plug-in cooler for car travel. Travel broadens the mind, and perhaps it has an effect on yeast growth. We feed it and water it, giving it a fifty-fifty mixture of filtered water and flour every week. In some ways, it is like a little pet. Not a terribly interactive pet, I have to say; it ranks well below guppies on that scale.

You can't even get its attention by tapping on its tub. I don't think I'd ever bother trying to show it competitively.

Catharine had scooped up some more of the lees and heaved them into the freezer for possible future beer experiments. Given how well the lees had done on flour, maybe if we started feeding them on wort, we could produce enough to make beer. Yeast is wildly prolific. Starting with a tiny packet of commercial dried yeast in December, I had a pound and a half of dark bubbling sludge by late January. Even as it sat in the refrigerator, it was busy reproducing, pushing up the lid on its tub. If present trends continued, I calculated, I'd have more than nine hundred pounds by year's end.

Freezing the lees had seemed sensible, but as we learned from reading Papazian and White, this kills the yeast, unless it has been mixed with glycerol beforehand. We keep pizza dough with live yeast in it frozen for months and months at a time, but the length of time this yeast had been stashed had certainly killed it.

Working the cider lees up into usable beer yeast would not be possible. But maybe, just maybe, we could mimic the bakers and brewers of old and use Catharine's sourdough starter, derived from the same cider lees, to ferment beer.

When it had come to planting my barley and hops, a lot of my reading had consisted of a mélange of contradictions and wish fulfillment—I sometimes thought that the writers were telling me not so much what was true, but what they fervently wished were the case—or worse, what they thought I wanted to hear. A little part of me thanked them for their consideration; mostly, though, I damned them.

Now I faced a new challenge. The more I read about working with yeast, the more one fact became clear: it just can't be done. The yeast was too vulnerable, the forces of bacterial evil arrayed against it too powerful. Every mote of dust was a bomb aimed directly at it, the average kitchen a festering swamp of contagion, little better than the open sewers of a medieval town. A rank amateur had a better chance of replacing the spent fuel rods in a nuclear reactor than he did of breeding up yeast successfully.

But, really, what did we have to lose? Papazian's book shows how to make a rig to help culture yeast from the lees off a batch of beer you've just brewed. Basically, it's a beer bottle with some sort of rubber stopper in the end, with a plastic hose attached. You run the hose into a glass of water. Like the "blow hose" running from the fermentation tank to the water-filled bucket at Lake of Bays, this rig lets the carbon dioxide escape but keeps out air and invasive yeasts and bacteria. You fill the bottle with malt, some hops and boiled water, stick in your yeast and attach the blow hose. Really, it's a miniature fermenter.

Papazian washes and then sterilizes his beer bottle, as far as I can make out, by heating particularly vulnerable spots like the mouth with a lighter. We were using plastic bottles but figured we could sterilize one pretty effectively by putting it in the dishwasher. It melted. We cleaned another bottle using our sterilizing powder, filled it with a mixture of malt, water, hops and a little of the sourdough starter, then tucked in a plastic hose and wrapped the mouth with tape to make it airtight. At the same time, just for the hell of it, we put some malt, water and hops in a bowl with the starter and covered it with plastic wrap.

The elaborate bottle experiment sat on the sideboard for about ten days, like some sort of bizarre centerpiece. In the meantime, the sample we had set up in the bowl seemed to be fermenting, but in the end, all it did was go really sour. We were also a little dubious about whether our more complex experiment was working: When we had poked the hose into the glass of water, the water rode up inside it a few inches. Sometimes, when we looked at the water inside the clear hose, the level seemed to have moved, as though it was being forced out by carbon dioxide. But this was barely perceptible and could just as easily have been wish fulfillment.

When we finally cracked it, unbelievably, we had beer. Cloudy as hell but unmistakably beer. Our sourdough bread yeast had started eating malt.

WHAT THE YEAST could do once, it could do again. We could build it up to take on larger brewing jobs and recycle it numerous times (in the same way that the commercial yeast that we had used to make what we came to call "Dog's Tongue Porter" went into our "Mocha Chocolate Valentine's Day Stout" and the first batch of "Ode to Spring," our "bière ordinaire," a straightforward ale we brewed exclusively for drinking as opposed to experimenting).

But what exactly could we create with it? Up to this point we had been imposing recipes on our ingredients.

If we wanted an ale or a porter, we found a recipe, then found the ingredients to match it (subject to a little improvisation). When I decided that a brown ale was the way to go, I knew producing it was going to be a little inexact given the rough and ready nature of our raw ingredients, but whatever recipe I found in a book or online would give me some guidance. A shift was happening. Our ingredients, or one of them in particular, would impose the beer on us.

It quickly became obvious that not just any beer style would work with the wild yeast. After our first yeast experiment, we tried out the yeast on some of the wort from our Mocha Chocolate Valentine's Day Stout, putting it in our fancy fermenting rig, and then setting it on the kitchen pass-through wrapped in a towel with a lamp trained on the bottle to encourage it to ferment.

When we decanted this, it had definitely fermented. And it was also definitely foul. Featuring chocolate and coffee, our Mocha Chocolate Valentine's Day Stout was as close as beer could get to being a true girlie drink—all it was missing was a little umbrella. Cloyingly sweet (and we had actually throttled back on the chocolate and left out the suggested vanilla altogether), this was not a recipe that worked with the slightly sour taste produced by our wild yeast.

I had always thought of beer as having two fundamental schools—British and German. Go along the British path and you get your ales, your stouts and your porters. Follow the German path and you get lagers. It's a common-enough belief, I think, but it's inaccurate. There is a third European school of brewing, an unusual one that is, in some ways, far more interesting than the British or German traditions.

Normally, when we think of Belgium, we think only of their waffles and their sprouts, ignoring all the while what they wash those down with: their beer. The Belgians brew using wheat, and they brew using fruit. Most daringly, they brew using wild yeast. Brewers in the area around Brussels, in the Senne Valley, have developed numerous wild yeast beers over the centuries. After they have brewed a wort (usually a mixture of malted barley and wheat), they leave it to cool in large open vats—often with the shutters of their breweries thrown wide to let whatever is floating around out there drift in. All sorts of microorganisms end up in their beers, the most significant of which is *Brettanomyces bruxellensis*.

Brettanomyces is another genus of yeast, close to but not the same as *Saccharomyces*. This particular strain produces beers that have quite a sour taste, often likened to cherries or lemon, and an aroma that is variously compared to, as one beer maker phrased it, "bad feet or good cheese." These yeasts are airborne, but the other place you commonly find them is on the skins of fruit. Such as the apples we had used to make our cider. So it seemed a good bet that we had captured some strain of *Brettanomyces*.

Our wild yeast, then, pretty much required us to make a sour beer. In recent years, as craft beer drinkers have become more sophisticated in their tastes and brewers have kept looking for something new to attract their fancy, Belgian brews have become more popular. We hadn't planned on it, but we would definitely be tapping into the zeitgeist by brewing a sour beer.

A sour fruit beer, I thought. There were a couple of reasons for this. We felt that the sourness of the yeast might work well with the sourness of the fruit. Note: sourness, not sweetness. Fruit beers confuse people. I think they summon up the idea of something like a cooler—those alcoholic versions of soda pop aimed at what I would charitably call "inexperienced" palates. But they're not like that. The yeast takes care of most of the sugars by turning them into alcohol. As an example of how that works, we had already made beer using maple syrup. Added to the primary fermenter, it isn't cloying. The yeast eats the sugars, leaving a crisp, dry flavor. Like maple syrup without the sweetness. Similarly, if you make a fruit beer with cherries, what you are left with is the essence of cherry—minus almost all the sugar. It sounds crazy, but once you taste it, you understand.

Flavor and tradition (many Belgian beers are fruit beers) weren't my only reasons for making a fruit beer. Our yeast was another factor. When it came to fermenting, I figured it needed all the help it could get. If it had survived by feeding on the sugars in fruit, let's give it fruit. Our two gallons of "Pinko," as we called our first wild yeast beer for reasons that will become obvious in a few more words, contained two pounds of rhubarb and cherries. As a further fermentation insurance policy, I tossed in six ounces of dextrose and four of maple syrup—plenty of varied material, I figured, for the yeast to work with. When it came to the grain, I opted for malt extract. Uninspired, perhaps, but I didn't want to take the chance that the yeast would have to deal with an imperfectly converted all-grain batch. I wanted a recipe that would, as much as possible, make things easy for my unicellular pal.

I had recently hived off some of the sourdough starter to use as beer yeast. One Thursday night, I took it out of the refrigerator, put it into a plastic tub and fed it a mixture of water and flour, just as though I was planning to make bread out of it. Then I put the tub on a beam above the stairs to the first floor with the lid askew. Thanks to the big gas fireplace on our ground floor, this is the warmest spot in our house. By morning, it had expanded nicely and there were big thick bubbles in it—it looked the way pancake batter does when it is just starting to cook.

Brewing fruit beer, at least using the recipe we had worked up, is not all that different from conventional brewing—in fact, the fruit doesn't go into the brew until the secondary fermentation. The biggest single difference was how lightly hopped it was. Rather than the typical three infusions, at the beginning of the boil, in the middle and finally at the end, the recipe called for just two. They were small ones at that, one at the beginning of the boil and the other at the end. I used Cascade hops, thinking that their citrusy flavor might work well in a fruit beer. Finally, putting my yeast tub on my digital scale, I scooped out six ounces of the goo with a sterilized steel spoon and pitched it into the wort. The gravity was 1.065, which suggested the final brew would be fairly strong—about 6.5 percent alcohol by volume.

If, that is, this wild yeast behaved like a commercial one. When brewers talk about the ability of yeast to convert sugars to alcohol, they mention what they call its attenuation. They express this as a percentage. A yeast that has an attenuation rate of 80 percent can convert 80 percent of the sugars in wort to alcohol. The attenuation is worked out by comparing the original and the final gravity of a brew, among other things. Of course, I didn't have those stats.

I also had no idea how quickly it would get to work, or how fast it would be finished. As I have mentioned, the lag time (to use the technical term) with commercial yeasts between when you pitch them and when they get to work is generally a few hours. We had to go away right after I pitched, so even if I had used a conventional yeast, it wouldn't have got going by the time we walked out the door.

In line with my usual method, I stashed the fermenter inside the front door, on the hard tile floor next to the gas fireplace. There's a little half wall between the door and the fire, and I tucked the big plastic tub wrapped in a towel in there to keep it warm. When we got back to the house several days later, I sat down on the floor cross-legged in front of the tub and fixed the air lock with a steady gaze.

I waited. And waited. (*Well*, I thought, *it just isn't happening. It*—)

Blunk.

A single bubble forced its way out of the air lock. Followed about a minute later by (*blunk*) another.

And so it went, hour after hour, day after day.

The rate of fermentation slowed, but only very gradually. This behavior was different from industrial yeast, which blips like crazy for about four days and then goes quiet, but I didn't see it as a bad thing. The bigger danger with wild yeast, I learned, was what are called "stuck" fermentations. These are exactly what they sound like. At some point, the yeast just stops converting sugar into alcohol. One common cause of stuck brews is the alcohol itself. It may sound paradoxical, but alcohol is fatal to yeast. That is one of the reasons why there are no fermented beverages with an alcohol content much above 13 percent by volume—that's all yeast can stand; to make it stronger, you need to use distillation. Over time, yeasts used in making beer and wine have been bred to withstand higher and higher levels of alcohol. Wild yeasts aren't as tolerant, so much lower levels of alcohol can be fatal to them. The acids that yeasts produce can also damage them.

By the time my yeast was bubbling only once every two and half minutes or so, I decided it might be wise to switch Pinko to the secondary fermenter. This switch would let me add the fruit and also get the brew off any of the bacteria and dead yeast that was building up on the bottom of the fermenter. The gravity at this point was 1.036, so it had dropped a fair bit, though it was still foamy and tasted slightly sweet.

In preparation for the switch to the secondary fermenter, I chopped up the rhubarb and added the frozen cherries and some water. I boiled this mixture at 160 degrees Fahrenheit, which helped soften it up as well as kill any potentially harmful bacteria. I poured the syrupy, pulpy mixture into the carboy using a funnel. The beer took on a pleasant pink tinge, which in turn gave the brew its name. Interestingly, after I added the fruit, fermentation seemed to pick up again. Not by a lot, admittedly, but noticeably. Slow but steady seemed to be the rule with this wild yeast. I learned later, too, that unlike ale yeast, which ferments on the top of beer, and lager yeast, which sits at the bottom, wild yeast diffuses throughout the liquid. So when I switched the brew from the primary to the secondary fermenter, most of the yeast went along. (And truth be told, wild yeast ferments so slowly—it just keeps glugging along at the same speed for weeks—that there is no great difference between primary and secondary fermentation.)

By the beginning of May, Pinko seemed to have settled down enough to bottle.

PINKO WORKED. IT was sour, to be sure, but this wasn't a sign of failure. It was a key element in the taste that combined really well with the cherries and the rhubarb. This was a refreshing, and refreshingly different, beer, a perfect sip for the summer. And it only improved with time, growing progressively tastier and more complex.

So if it came to it, my perfect keg might be a fruit beer. At least I knew that a fruit beer would work with my yeast. Although the big challenge would be finding the fruit to make such a beer at our farm. We had rhubarb, and plenty of it, but not much of anything else. Apples, yes, but I didn't want to make cider, really. There were a few other fruit trees, cherries and wild plums, but generally they didn't produce enough fruit in a typical year. That left juniper berries, great if I wanted a beer that tasted like gin.

Then I had one of those serendipitous experiences that sometimes seemed to define this whole project.

As well as writing about beer, and making it, I sometimes also talk about it. On the 2012 May long weekend, I was part of a beer and whiskey event for the local United Way held in a theater in downtown Kingston. The idea was you paid to get in, and then you could sample the wares of various distilleries and craft brewers. There was an expert to talk about Scotch, and I was doing the chore for beer. The Scotch guy had a kilt—but I think my PowerPoint show trumped his skirt. As well as delivering my famed talk, Five Beers over Canada, I was also supposed to lead people on guided tastings, taking them from one craft brewer to another and explaining what it was they were noticing in various beers. The idea was that I would do this twice, once at four and then again at six, although as it turned out, everyone was too far gone by six.

My group at four comprised an older guy, his son-in-law, an amateur brewer and his girlfriend and her two very pretty female Mexican friends from their graduate kinesiology program who reacted to most of the beers by scowling and sticking out their tongues. (It's a long way from light Mexican lager to full-on craft beer.) I decided to start them off at the Mill Street brewing table. Joel Manning, the brewmaster, had been a great help to me when I was writing my first beer book. He's a creative brewer, so I am always interested to see what he's getting up to.

Earlier I had scoped out a beer here called Ambre de la Chaudière. Now was my chance to try it.

My God. Talk about truth in a bottle. Great flavor. Great balance. Mr. Live Yeast was in there, but he had been tamed. This was Belgian, but not quite. As I sipped it, my beer tastes were changing. I'd been fairly ambivalent about the Belgians—but here, here, was a live yeast beer I could believe in.

In fact, it was a style known as bière du garde, which literally translated means "beer for keeping." It isn't Belgian; it's French, from the Pas de Calais region—the flat bit of northern France where so much of the First World War was fought. Having said that, bière du garde is also very much like a Belgian beer known as a saison. In both cases, this was a beer made from grain in the colder months and then laid down in storage. Farm workers would drink it in the summer to quench their thirst as they labored. It was bottle-conditioned instead of aged in a wooden cask. Some of the descriptions of the flavor that I read—"barnyard," for example—suggested that at least some versions were brewed with strains of wild yeast. Whatever the case, I figured never mind fruit, we could make something like this.

It might not be historically accurate, not for my corner of the world, but it might well be fantastic beer.

THIS WAS OUR first attempt at using our own wild yeast in a beer. And our first attempt at a fruit beer. We took our lead from information we found in the excellent book *The Homebrewer's Garden*. At this point, we had no idea what exactly we were dealing with in our yeast—it was wild, all right, but beyond that we knew nothing.

The Belgians brew a number of fruit beers, notably what is called Kriek (made from cherries), using lambic yeast—a fancy way of saying whatever drifts in. Because we weren't sure what was going to happen, or indeed if anything was going to happen, we kept the recipe for this one very simple—just malt extract and only one kind of hop, the Cascade hops we had grown, and just two infusions. In contrast, Belgian lambics usually contain a fair whack of malted wheat, and they use hops that have been sitting around for years, which gives them a "cheesy" odor. (Dirty feet, cheesy, barnyard—for someone who hasn't tasted them, it is difficult to imagine why people would drink Belgian beer, let alone be fanatic about it.)

If you can't lay your hands on wild yeast, any conventional ale yeast would probably do the job. That would give you a fruit beer, all right, but not the proper sour taste that a wild yeast would. The estimable White Labs in California produce two types of *Brettanomyces* for home use that you can order from better brewery supply places. Or you can just put this beer outside, uncovered, for a day or so and see what happens.

GRAIN BILL

2.6 lbs Malt extract

0.5 lbs Malted wheat

2 lbs Fruit (cherries and rhubarb)

6 oz Dextrose

4 oz Maple syrup

(Total 5 lbs 11.6 oz)

HOPS BILL

0.3 oz Cascade (60 minutes)

0.3 oz Cascade (0 minutes)

YEAST

About 6 oz of starter (our wild yeast)

OG: 1.065

FG: 1.022

Method: Heat 0.5 U.S. gallons of water to 170 degrees Fahrenheit. Add crushed wheat and steep for 30 minutes. Sparge at 168 degrees Fahrenheit, bringing volume up to 0.8 gallons. Add malt extract, dextrose, syrup and water to make 1.8 gallons. Boil for 60 minutes, adding hops as indicated. Remove from heat. Bring the total volume to 1.5 gallons. Strain. Cool to 70 degrees Fahrenheit and pitch yeast. When ready to transfer to secondary fermenter, stew fruit in 160 degrees Fahrenheit water for 15 minutes and cool. Add it to secondary and rack wort onto it. Be patient, be very patient.

Eight

MALTING WALTZILDA

THERE ARE CERTAIN activities in this world—brain surgery and burlesque dancing come readily to mind—that require both innate talent and a lot of study. There is no room for amateurs.

Malting is the same. We had to learn how to malt if we really wanted to make beer from scratch. So we learned how to malt. And honestly? I think we got more than half-good at it.

Not that this distinction is actually worth much. Generally, with beer making, anything you do yourself is better than anything the pros can do. But not malting. Never again will I malt.

Throughout my story, I have been talking about malt but without ever bothering to explain in much detail what it is or, more importantly, what malting is. I'll try to keep this explanation as nontechnical as possible. And as my botanical knowledge is limited to my failed barley crop and growing a bean plant in grade four, that won't be difficult.

Here we go. Malting works with the natural action of a seed. A very large part of a seed is starch. Think of this starch as stored food. Once the seed begins germinating, it triggers the production of certain enzymes (called diastase) in the kernel, and these enzymes in turn begin converting the stored starches into sugars (mostly glucose and maltose, at least in the case of barley, but there are others) that the plant will need to keep it going while it grows roots and a stem and before it can begin to feed itself with photosynthesis.

In malting, you turn on germination by soaking the barley seed until it sprouts—this is something familiar to anyone who has ever sprouted beans or whatever. But here's the neat part. Having started germination by soaking the barley, you then stop it. By drying and heating the barley. The glory of malting is that when you take this malted barley, grind it up, add water and raise the temperature to between 150 and 160 degrees, the diastolic enzymes in the malt become very active and, hey presto, convert the starches to sugars.

Okay, I should note that not all malts have these enzymes. The pale two-row malts used as the basis of craft beers do, and the six-row version favored by what I guess could be called "mainstream" brewers do as well. But a lot of what brewers call specialty malts—the crystal malts, the black malts and so on—do not. That's because producing them requires higher temperatures to make them crystalline or turn them dark, and that much heat destroys the enzymes. The enzymes are in grass seeds (and remember barley is a grass) located in the outer part of the starchy part of the seed. One of the nifty things about barley, however, is that it contains so much of the enzymes—a wall three cells thick surrounding the starch, whereas most grasses have just a single thickness. So if you add a specialty malt to your brew, it doesn't matter that it lacks the enzymes itself as long as there is pale two row in there as well. The diastolic enzymes in it can convert the specialty malt's starches as well.

This quality has also made it possible for breweries to make beer using six-row barley with significant amounts of adjuncts—rice and corn are the two most common examples. The diastolic enzymes in six row, as in two row, can convert all their own starches to sugars, and have plenty left over to convert any other starches that happen to be to hand. Historically, six-row barley wasn't regarded as being very good for brewing. It had more of the enzymes but less usable starch. But once someone figured out these excess enzymes could ferment other grains, six row became the commercial malting barley of choice in North America.

It all sounds pretty straightforward. In fact, it *is* pretty straightforward. But the problem was trying to find simple instructions on how to malt. If what I had read on growing barley had been plain wrong, and the expert opinion on working with yeast made it sound downright impossible, malting presented me with a wealth of instructions, all of which seemed contradictory.

I always used to enjoy it when I'd see a review of some band in the paper, Stig Torpor and the Vindaloos come readily to mind, and then a few days later a letter would show up (this happens on the Web, too) that would almost always start with "I can't believe I was at the same Stig Torpor and the Vindaloos show as your reviewer the other night..." then go on to describe a virtual alternative reality from that put forth in the review. I kept thinking of that phenomenon when I started trying to learn how to malt, because we found ourselves sifting our way through a morass of contrary explanations with so little in common they might well have been describing activities as different as baking bread and cold-rolling steel.

To begin, soak the barley for an hour or two. No, soak it for four hours. For eight hours. For three days. Aerate it. Don't aerate it. Dry it out. Don't dry it out. Couch it (let it rest) with carbon dioxide. Get rid of the carbon dioxide. Seal it in a bag. Leave it open. The finished malt will weigh two-thirds the weight of the original barley. There will be no difference. But perhaps best of all: "Techniques will differ according to your malting philosophy." Of course, my malting philosophy: "I used to do a lot of Aristotelian malting, but my approach recently has become increasingly Heideggerian."

Back before Christmas when we were trying to figure out whether the wild yeast we had in our refrigerator could make beer, Catharine took some of the barley we had sitting in burlap bags on our ground floor, soaked it, folded it into a piece of damp paper towel and then put it on a little dish in the kitchen The idea was to see whether we could get it to start germinating—that essential first step on the way to malting. It so happened that we could. Now the question became how to get from those four sprouts to a finished product we could make beer with.

"OF ALL THE steps in microbrewing, micromalting would be the hardest."

I was sitting talking to Duane Falk, a tall, bearded professor emeritus at the University of Guelph. Falk's linoleum-floored office was in the Crop Science Building, a bleak modernist concrete legacy of the 1960s located along an idyllic pathway called Reynolds Walk that ran the length of the university campus. Well, idyllic in summer, I have no doubt. But I was visiting on a dreary, snowless winter day. To find his office, I had walked past room after room filled with all manner of crops growing under fluorescent lights—I thought of it as one enormous legal grow op. All that green made a nice contrast to the gray-brown outdoors.

Given the contradictory nature of everything I had read about malting, I thought it might be wiser to seek out and talk to experts. But there was one big challenge to malting, and that was what Professor Falk was alluding to.

Simply put, malting is a big business. In terms of revenues, to be sure, but also in the scale of production. There is really no such thing as a mom-and-pop malting operation. Even the smallest independent maltsters (and there aren't many of them) think in terms of tons. If I wanted to learn how to malt properly, I was going to have to start with a complex industrial process and figure out how to simplify and scale it down.

I started to realize this with the very first person I talked to, Bruce French, the director of malting and technical services at Canada Malting. Canada produces 1 million tons of malt annually. We are one of the world's leading exporters of malt, and Canada Malting accounts for nearly half of the national total. Headquartered in Calgary (all the barley they use is grown out west), they have a malting plant there, others in Thunder Bay and Montreal, and grain elevators scattered across western Canada. "We ship all over the world," French said, "via bulk vessels to Japan, South America, Central America and all over the Caribbean."

If French emphasized one point about the big malting operations, it was consistency. Barley is a natural product, and like everything natural, it is far from uniform. But uniformity is precisely what brewers demand. The market for malt is fragmenting, like the market for everything nowadays, with craft brewers at one end, discount beers at the other and the traditional middle being squeezed out. The craft brewers are looking for varieties of two row, whereas "the big guys need malts that are high in proteins and enzymes." Six row, in other words. But big or small, when it comes to malt, said French, "they all want one thing: that it function as expected and that it be consistent."

French was able to lead me through the steps of malting—generally stated, they are steeping, germinating and kilning—but the scale Canada Malting works on was far removed from anything I could imagine. When they germinate, for example, they soak a load of barley a meter deep in an enormous tank. This rests on a perforated floor through which they pump air. They can exactly maintain the temperature of the air and the water. When it comes to the kilning, they don't heap their barley quite as high, just three-quarters of a meter, but they are able to dry it precisely at progressively higher temperatures. They can gauge changes that an amateur like me cannot. They were happy only when their product turned out the same way every time; I'd be happy to have mine turn out at all.

That's what had brought me to Professor Falk's office the day after I spoke to Bruce French. The University of Guelph, and its predecessor the Ontario Agricultural College, can claim a very honorable place in the world of barley and malting. Back in 1910, the college introduced OAC 21, a strain of six-row barley that Charles Zavitz developed over the course of several decades. (The strain is called 21 because it was the twenty-first row produced in their search for a superior malting barley.) Before this time, the preferred Canadian malting varieties had all been British and French strains of two-row barley. OAC 21 was an excellent malting variety and extremely well suited for brewing American beers. It was soon widely adopted out west and, Falk told me, essentially launched the Canadian malting industry. A highly adaptable barley, it has been crossed with many other strains over the years, and these descendants are still widely grown today.

When I had first e-mailed Professor Falk, he had responded that he had "some experience with malting." When we met, I learned that this was somewhat of an understatement. In addition to his academic credentials (degrees from the Universities of Montana and Guelph, including two, I was delighted to learn, "in wheat"), Falk worked for a number of years at the largest malting company in New Zealand, where part of his job was to visit the breweries every few weeks to do quality control. I liked, too, what he had to say when I told him about my experiences with wild yeast and its unusual slow-by-steady fermentation: "It concentrates on surviving, not fermenting." He suggested that I could build it up for more brewing by feeding it a regular diet of rye flour, advice I have followed successfully ever since.

If I had to reduce what Falk told me about how to malt to just two words, I'd pick "time" and "weight." "You want to wet it slowly," he said. To start off, you would steep your barley in water for a couple of hours, at about fifty-four to sixty degrees Fahrenheit. "You must," he told me, "aerate the water." Otherwise, the barley will die.

"Then give it an eight-hour rest, but keep it humid." During the rest, you drain off the water and just let the barley sit—taking care not to let it dry out. Follow this with another couple of hours of steeping. Then let it rest for eight hours and finally give it, he said, "a final sprinkle."

"You want the barley to go from being about 12–14 percent moisture to about 45 to 47 percent. Forty-five is the ideal." That's where weight comes in. To monitor your barley's moisture content, you weigh it before you begin and then repeatedly during this whole cycle of soaking and resting.

You also watch for the chits, the small white beginning of the roots, as they begin to poke through the end of the seed. Once they appear, you can begin to think about the germination.

To know when to start the final stage, kilning, Falk told me you needed to look at the acrospire. This is the thin nascent shoot from which the top of the plant will develop, and it grows under the skin of the barley kernel in the opposite direction to the chits or rootlets. "When one-quarter of the acrospires have reached the end of the seed, it is ready for the drying or kilning process," he explained. "Then you want to reduce moisture. Down to 2–4 percent." You do this by using lots of moving air and bumping up the temperature in small increments, which slowly dries the barley out. As it dries, of course, it gets lighter and lighter. "The barley will lose 8 to 10 percent of its [original] weight during the malting because it is burning up some of its starch for growth during the germination process" he said. "The higher the loss, the greater the enzyme [available]."

THE BUBBLER WHIRRED away in the five-gallon pot on the floor in the back of the car, its persistent *zzzzzzz* a faint counterpoint to the sound of the air conditioner and the rumble of the car's tires on the road. We were en route home from the farm with a load of germinating barley.

The bubbler was one of those devices that you see sitting in the bottom of tanks of tropical fish, sometimes disguised as a treasure chest or a deep-sea diver. Ours was far more mundane, just a round, flat disk five inches or so in diameter and about an inch deep with an air hose and an electrical cord running off it. It filled me with apprehension. There was nothing magical about it in itself, and it was the only piece of specialized "equipment" that we had to buy, ever, but it represented a complex, time-consuming process—one we had no guarantee would work.

After dinner at the farm on Friday night, I put four ounces of my practice barley into a deep roasting pan and covered the barley with well water, and then set it on the butcher-block counter in the farm's kitchen. I cleared away some of the barley from the bottom of the pan with my hand and stuck in my bubbler, which I weighed down with a small, smooth piece of quartz. Then I plugged it in, releasing a steady stream of bubbles to aerate the water. Around eleven, just before going to bed, I unplugged the bubbler, drained the water off my barley and spooned it out onto a cookie sheet lined with paper towels. I put this in a cold oven overnight—to protect it from mice.

In the morning, before I returned the barley to the bubbling waters, I weighed it. It was now six ounces—a 50 percent gain. By four twenty in the afternoon, the chits were starting to appear. I drained the barley, scooped it out and weighed it again. Eight and a half ounces. It had more than doubled in weight.

Next, I dumped the barley into a colander. In the farm's utility (that is, junk) room, I found a five-gallon pot used to make preserves. It was pretty much identical to my brewing kettle. I added a couple of inches of water and put the colander into the pot, resting on a folding wire device that I think was intended to hold jars for canning. This kept the colander well clear of the water and let me slip the bubbler in underneath to help keep the barley damp and chase off carbon dioxide.

I put the setup in the dark, cool utility room. The lid was slightly ajar because of the protruding electrical cord for the bubbler, so I covered the pot loosely with a towel to keep all the light out. Too much light would dry it out. After that, I pretty much left it alone, except to turn the barley with a large slotted plastic spoon every few hours. By Sunday afternoon, more chits had appeared and a few had even sprouted into rootlets, pale little triads that would ultimately turn into roots. We took out one of the barleycorns, cut it open and, under a magnifying glass borrowed from the farm's venerable two-volume *Oxford English Dictionary,* could make out the acrospires just starting. The barley needed a few more hours to develop these, so we kept it germinating in the car all the way home.

For the home maltster, the big challenge with drying or kilning malt is keeping it going at relatively low temperatures—lower, in fact, than most ovens can produce. You want to do it for a time, we reckoned a few hours, at around 122 degrees Fahrenheit, then step it up to 140 and finally top out around 167. We decided to put the barley into our wall oven, without turning it on, and see if we could come up with any low-temperature heat sources. Initially we had two desk lamps in with the barley, with our digital meat thermometer stuck into the heaped grain to let us monitor the temperature. Just like the heat source in the old Kenner Easy-Bake Oven. The problem was that, just like the Easy-Bake, our oven never got quite warm enough. The temperature would crawl up to about 118 degrees and then sit there.

Monday morning, I had to go out for a meeting. As I climbed the stairs to our kitchen on my return, I could hear a faint whirring—a different whirring from the bubbler, though, more like the buzzing of a large swarm of flies. Catharine had put a hair dryer into the oven in place of the desk lamps. This seemed to make a difference. And it had another advantage. When you are kilning, you not only need to worry about temperature; you need to keep an eye on air circulation. But they have an inverse relationship. To ensure the malt dries properly, you want a lot of air circulating at first, when the temperature is low, but less when it gets warmer. Thanks to the hair dryer, the malt reached the right temperature and the air kept circulating.

The bulk of the day, and it took hours, consisted of drying while monitoring the digital thermometer to make sure the barley was neither too cold nor too hot, but just right. To stop it from overheating and help the air circulate, we propped open the oven door using a wine cork and some masking tape. By shifting the cork up and down in the door, we could widen or narrow the opening and control the temperature inside the oven fairly well. Every so often, we would pull the barley out to see how it was drying. Part of that was visual. We took a couple of grains and put them in a white bowl. If we could see some beads of moisture on the dish, we needed to keep drying. The other test was to weigh it. We knew how much we had started with and we knew how much it had expanded to at its maximum weight. Now we started to go in the opposite direction. This first stage was intended to reduce the moisture content from about 48 percent to 23 percent.

(Barley begins at about 14 percent moisture content.) That meant taking the weight back down to around six ounces. After that, we put it back in at 140 to 160 degrees Fahrenheit until it got to about 12 percent moisture left. At this point, it weighed about five ounces. The hair dryer was fine at the lower temperatures, but when we boosted the temperature for the second stage of kilning, it began giving these sad pathetic surges—unh-*hunh*—every now and again. The poor old hair dryer wasn't designed for such effort—as Catharine put it, it would be like using this single hair dryer to do all the contestants' hair for the Miss South Carolina pageant.

Fortunately, for the final stage, we could abandon the hair dryer and turn on the oven at its lowest temperature. By this point, the barley was beginning to smell like malt, a beautiful, sweet toasty aroma. In fact, the whole house smelled like the malting plant that used to sit on the Toronto waterfront when I was a kid and was, for me, the defining smell of my hometown. It was beginning to look like malt, too, nice light brown kernels a quarter inch long, if not quite as uniform and as beautiful as the commercial variety. We weighed it and we had three and three-eighths ounces of malt. From an initial four ounces. I had wondered if the professionals had any sort of test that let them know when their malt was done. Probably, I figured, something involving calipers and digital displays. I had e-mailed Duane Falk and asked him. "They take a grain," he e-mailed me back, "and bite it to see if it's brittle." I had some commercial two row sitting around, so I took a few grains and nibbled them. Then I nibbled ours. It nibbled exactly like commercial malt. More importantly, it had malt's slightly biscuity sweetness.

Probably the most important lesson we learned about malting was that to do it properly, watching the malt was more important than blindly depending on the times. I think we were correct to do our initial schedule of four hours soaking, eight hours sitting, four hours soaking, but the real key was to watch for the formation of the chits. Once that is well under way, it is ready to start the germinating—no matter what times you think you should follow. Having said that, germinating is one place where I think time is relatively more straightforward—seventy-two hours seemed right. After that, though, it is more a case of warming and weighing. So watching, weighing and warming—the three Ws of malting.

ONCE WE STARTED malting, I assumed we could pump it out in larger quantities, say a couple of pounds at a time. A five-gallon brew would take around ten pounds. I figured that with weekly maltings, it wouldn't be too long, a matter of a month or so, before we'd have a pile of malt to play with. We could even use my handpicked crop and get started on the final brew. As always, reality turned out to be a little more complicated.

When I had talked to Bruce French at Canada Malting, he told me about Don McOuatt, a retired executive from Canada Malting who lived in Kingston. French said he himself still called Don from time to time when he had technical questions. "Maybe," he had joked, "he'll even show you how to malt."

Catharine and I met Don for lunch in one of our local watering holes. He was a snowy-haired, erect man in his early eighties, wearing jeans, a barge cap and a faded red canvas shirt, who was kind enough to lend us his copy of *Practical Brewing*. Like Falk and French, he could explain the principles of industrial malting—the need for consistency and so on. But perhaps because he was older, he also had a connection to an earlier era of malting. In the 1960s, when Canada Malting was expanding internationally, he made frequent trips to England, where small local maltsters were still doing it the way they had for centuries: heaping the malting grain on a concrete or stone floor to germinate, turning it with basswood shovels, opening and shutting windows to control the temperature. Malting that way still had a bit of art, rather than science, about it. And so was the step Don added to the malting process that no one else had touched on. Once we had finished malting, he told us (and I was heartened because that seemed to imply that he thought we could do it), we had to age the malt. Generally, he said, "for about six weeks."

"No one," he said, "quite knows why. But if a brewmaster got a batch that hadn't been aged, he could tell—and he wouldn't be happy."

I suspect that with most modern maltsters this step is unstated but implicit—their malt sits around for weeks after they finish it and before they deliver it. And probably for weeks after that at their customers' breweries. But I had been sort of depending on just-in-time malting. The addition of the aging step would push the brewing of our perfect keg a bit into the future. If we started malting in June, producing a few pounds at a time, we wouldn't be doing any brewing with our own malt exclusively until at least August.

Or even later, as it turned out.

We needed to get busy. On June 7, I started just over two pounds of barley, malting at one thirty in the afternoon. I used the same equipment and techniques as with four ounces but just scaled up the barley. By Saturday morning, June 9, it had swollen to nearly twice its original weight.

At this point, I transferred it to the colander in the five-gallon pot, which I put just inside the front door, tucked in the cool little space where I always put my carboy, and covered with a towel. By Tuesday morning, June 12, at eight thirty, it would be ready to start the kilning. We had to go to Toronto for a couple of days, but I figured we could leave the barley bubbling away because the weather was relatively cool. We would be back well before germination was over on Tuesday. Well, that was the theory, anyway.

I'd always known that in the olden days brewers didn't make beer in the summer, without ever quite remembering why. I soon found out. We returned from Toronto on Monday, laden with a few leftovers from our move that we had to pick up—pretty typical stuff: an ice chipper, a vintage pond yacht handmade by Catharine's grandfather, and a bell jar containing a statue of the biblical Ruth and Naomi (immortalized by Keats for hanging out "amid the alien corn").

I was a little concerned because the weather had changed, becoming hot and humid. As soon as I had unburdened myself of the bell jar, I popped the lid on my barley. Alien corn, indeed. It had sprouted—long, thin white slivers of mold. I had wanted the barley damp, but not the damp you get from an unseasonably hot and humid summer in June in the middle of North America.

Modern people think that somehow the weather and the seasons don't really affect what they do. And I guess they're right, to some extent, driving around in air-conditioned cars, living and working in climate-controlled environments. But let them attempt something like this, and the vagaries of the weather are paramount. An instant reminder of why, historically, people didn't brew in the summer months.

I reckoned it would be sometime after Labor Day before we could start malting again.

BUT WE COULD still make beer. As well as turning out five-gallon lots for our own consumption (Ode Reloaded followed Ode to Spring and was in turn followed by Triode), I was eager to see how well my own malted barley would work in an actual beer. I didn't have enough for even a two-gallon lot, nowhere near enough, but I could combine it with regular two-row malt and some malted wheat. It might be that my own malt wouldn't work all that well, but the commercial stuff would still get the job done. I combined these with our own Cascade and Nugget hops and, of course, our very own strain of wild yeast. We were getting very close to the final brew.

And into distinctly weird territory. Everything about "Wild Thang," as I named it, was odd. It seemed that the conversion of the starches in the malt to sugars, which the yeast would later convert into alcohol, never quite worked, no matter how careful I was about holding the wort at the correct temperature. Every time I did an iodine test, it showed that there were still unconverted starches. I had no choice but to move everything into the primary fermenter.

To do smaller brews, I had scored an empty two-gallon plastic tub from the local health food store, one of those containers that organic honey or peanut butter comes in. It opened by pulling on a long plastic strip. Once I opened it, however, I couldn't reseal it by snapping the lid back. Instead, I made it airtight, or tried to, by circling the lid several times with duct tape. Maybe the carbon dioxide was seeping out somewhere, because whenever I checked the air lock, nothing seemed to be happening, not a rattle or a bubble. There's a little cap inside the air lock so that water doesn't get into the beer. Even if you never see your brew actively bubble, the cap should slowly ride up over time. Instead, it sat unmoving, day after day.

When I shifted the beer to the secondary fermenter, I was relieved that it did seem to be fermenting. But I got freaked out by the beer's appearance. Beer at this stage often has a look akin to Wink or Fresca, one of those cloudy, grapefruit-based soft drinks. It always clears. But Wild Thang had what I noted in my work dairy at the time as a "distinctly cheesy vibe." It looked like you could spread it on bread. I sampled some when we bottled it. It didn't taste cheesy, but it was, as Catharine put it, "very, very Belgian" in taste and appearance. This was the first brew I had ever made that Catharine blanched at before tasting. And although it didn't look quite as odd as when it went into the secondary fermenter, it still had a strange milky appearance.

I let it sit in the bottles for more than a month behind the wine bottles and the power tools at the back of a cool closet on the first floor. By late August, I noticed that it had cleared. When I opened the initial bottle of Wild Thang, I had to say that on first drink it was just okay. But two nights later, I opened another, and it was great. Perhaps part of the challenge of brewing with wild yeast and odd homemade ingredients is that you can have such differences among bottles of the same brew. Regardless, that second one was dry and not at all sweet—tart, fruity but not sweet, not one bit sweet, which was a good thing. It didn't taste too strongly hopped either, which was weird because I had dry-hopped it, but the mouth feel was incredible. In a way, it was a bit like cider—but a cider that has grown up and faced a few disappointments. Cider with a secret, maybe.

Another of our beers for drinking, as opposed to experimenting on, was Ode to Spring. We ultimately brewed three versions of it: Ode to Spring, Ode Reloaded and, finally, Triode. Ode to Spring was a partial extract affair; Ode Reloaded was all-grain. The predominant grain we used was Maris Otter, a variety of two row developed in England in the 1960s that is very good for producing traditional British beers. I hadn't really planned it, but in this case it went particularly well with a Nottingham-style ale yeast and Brewer's Gold, a hop first developed in England in the 1930s. Brewer's Gold was one of the hop varieties that Quebec hop farmer Tim Wickens was kind enough to send me after I visited him. We found that the little bit of wheat makes for a lighter taste.

GRAIN BILL

9 lbs Maris Otter

11 oz Wheat malt

2 lbs Crystal malt

(Total 11 lbs 11 oz)

HOPS BILL

1 oz Brewer's Gold (50 minutes)

0.5 oz Cascade (10 minutes)

0.5 oz Cascade (0 minutes)

YEAST

Lallemand Danstar Nottingham Ale Yeast

OG: 1.055

FG: 1.016

Method: Follow instructions as in Bière Ordinaire (page 62); iodine test required.

Nine

ROLL OUT THE SEMI-DEMI-PIN

FROM THE BEGINNING of this project, I really wanted to make beer in a barrel. In fact, even before I knew much about the nuts and bolts of producing beer, I knew that I wanted to put it in a keg. Partly because, at first anyway, I thought it would be historically accurate. And beyond that, to be honest, it sounded so right. "Arr, maties, we'll tap a keg and then set sail for the high seas," and so forth.

I was, in fact, wrong. Words like "cask" and "keg," which I tended to treat as synonyms, are as much about function as the object. On the one hand, in beer lingo, if you are doing what I planned, which was to ferment the beer within a barrel, this is called cask-conditioning, and I think that by extension the vessel you would do it in would be a cask. And it need not be wood—your cask can be aluminum or plastic. Beers made this way are very mildly carbonated, and you have to draw them out of the cask with a hand pump traditionally called a beer engine. Whenever you hear people from the Campaign for Real Ale (CAMRA) in Great Britain talking about "real" ale, this kind of beer is what they mean.

On the other hand, kegged beer refers to beer that is fermented in large tanks, then shot full of carbon dioxide and pumped into bottles, cans or aluminum kegs. Hence "kegger," a party featuring one of those big metal barrels. The people from CAMRA might deny it, but lots of good—hell, great—beer is made this way. All those fantastic West Coast–style pale ales, for example. One other thing I learned: beer language is laden language. That goes even for the word "barrel," as we shall see.

To avoid these problems, let me call what I was looking for a "volume beer storage unit." Sadly, it's been almost sixty years since aluminum kegs replaced wooden ones, and they are getting fairly thin on the ground. A lot of them were sold off and turned into planters when the breweries switched over. I knew the brewery at Black Creek Pioneer Village used old whiskey kegs precisely because they couldn't lay their hands on enough of the real thing. On the Web I found a British company that was still manufacturing them, but they warned that they were not to be used for beer. They were intended essentially for decorating, the sort of thing you would scatter about your "Olde English" pub, along with the horse brasses, to give it a dollop of authenticity.

I did have leads on one or two collectors who might have wooden kegs to spare, but there were problems with that, too. Specifically, volume. Traditional "volume beer storage units" came in a variety of sizes. At the top end of the range you had the mighty tun, which held 216 imperial gallons. The next step below that was the butt, which held half that, followed by the hogshead, which contained 54 gallons. Smack in the middle was the barrel, a specific form of cask or keg holding 36 gallons, which can be a bit of a source of confusion given how we use the word generically. And just to muddy the water (or ale), American barrels are different from imperial ones—they hold 31 (smaller American) gallons. Below that there were ever smaller units: the kilderkin, the firkin (one of the best things about beer kegs was the nomenclature) and, last but by no means least, the pin, or as it is sometimes called when made out of plastic, the polypin (I'm not kidding). My problem was that even the smallest of these, the pin, held 4.5 imperial gallons, which was more beer than I figured I had the makings for. I needed something smaller, say, a demi-pin.

Back in the early days of my project, I had come across an incredible store called Adventures in Homebrewing on the outskirts of Detroit. I seemed to recall that they did barrels. In fact, they did. Not in many sizes, however. They didn't have a two-gallon job, but they did advertise an even smaller one that held about 1.2 gallons—what I guess you could call a semi-demi-pin. It wasn't perfect, but it was close. A sturdy little oak barrel, it was bound by brass rings and featured a cute little spigot. When I called them, they assured me that, yes, it was a real beer barrel. They didn't have it in stock, but the clerk told me they would order one from Minnesota for me. But he cautioned it might take a while: "Sometimes the barrel guy can be a little... mercurial."

WHEN THE WEATHER turned cooler after Labor Day, I made a load of what I thought of as conventional all-grain beer with store-bought yeast—that is, beer exclusively for drinking, not as an experiment—followed by another conventional brew a few weeks later. I thought of this as building my strategic beer reserve—my dream was to never buy commercial beer again.

Once it was cooler, we could also start thinking about malting again. And bringing in our crops. Back in the late spring, I had planted barley again. You aren't supposed to plant barley in the same field two years running, but as Harold pointed out, it hadn't really worked the first year, so it shouldn't be problem planting it again. As I had something like fifty pounds of barley seed left over from my first go-round with planting, it seemed wasteful not to use it. I planted two lots of barley, separated by a few weeks. The previous year, I had babied my crop and the barley had all died. So I decided to do the exact opposite this time. I did nothing for my crops. Nothing. Didn't weed, didn't worry about water, all with the result that this barley did way better than the previous year's. The first batch looked a little stressed—we had had a very dry summer—but the second lot, which we sowed pretty much just to keep down the weeds and use up an empty bit of field, looked really good. And, in fact, it gave me a fairly decent crop.

The hops had come back strong in the second year, too. Exceeded my expectations, in fact. By midsummer, they had all climbed right to the roof of the henhouse, and some of them were tentatively feeling their way well past there. I extended their lines by screwing two-by-twos to the fascia on their side of the henhouse and similar pieces on the fascia at the opposite end of the coop. Then I ran heavy brown twine between these to give the hops something to climb along. When I picked them in September, I got more than a pound of hops from my plants, mostly from the Cascade and Nugget. The first year I had picked them all individually, like grapes. This year, I didn't bother—I just cut down the vines and pulled the cones off. It wouldn't hurt them—hops are tough; cut them right down to the ground and they will come back the next year.

Last year, I had dried my hops for storage on the platform I had nicked from my neighbors' garbage and tacked a screen over. It had worked all right, but I had a better system in mind for this year. I had found a wobbly and badly oxidized aluminum-framed window screen tucked away in the henhouse—destined, I imagined, for the dump. In an upstairs bedroom at the farm, I created a drying rack by resting the screen on the edges of two chairs and spreading the hops over it. Then I put a fan on the nearby bookshelf—higher than the screen so that the air would move over the hops indirectly instead of blowing them all over the room. I cracked the window and tacked a towel over it so that no light could get in. Sunlight can destroy the volatile oils in hops and give them a skunky flavor. I left them overnight. In the morning, they had dried perfectly and opened up beautifully.

The same banged-up screen proved useful for malting as well. I tucked a space heater under the screen, spread my sodden barley on it, and then tossed a stiff polyester blanket over the chair backs, creating a sort of malting tent. This worked much better than the hair dryer in the oven. The heater had a rheostat, so we were able to control the temperature fairly precisely, too.

I had been a little worried that I let the barley bubble for too long. I got mixed up on the whole four hours soaking, eight hours resting, four hours soaking thing and left it immersed and bubbling all night. In the end, however, it didn't seem to matter. Which was a good thing because I made this malt with the barley I had personally harvested last fall over at Mike's farm in Quebec, and I didn't have a lot of it. Given that I had beaten it with a broom, picked the heads off by hand and winnowed it, I was astounded by how much crud was left in it. So I winnowed it again, using a slightly simpler technique than my earlier full-on Bollywood method. Standing outside on the porch in a good breeze, I grabbed big handfuls of barley and let it trickle through my fingers into a colander. This took some finessing—if the distance between the colander and my hand was too small, I ended up with a lot of chaff. If the distance was too great, most of the barley blew away. It felt like it was about three degrees outside, and I couldn't do this while wearing gloves, so my hands were in a real state after a couple of hours. Even this work hadn't quite done the job, so I spread out the barley in a large roasting pan and sorted through it manually. As I picked out what felt like my hundredth timothy seed, I had a revelation (or maybe an excuse): in the olden days, people would have accepted a much higher level of crud in winnowed barley. I was applying the assumptions of the industrial age to a preindustrial process. I needed to accept that any residual chaff and any small stones would simply add—no, make that *impart*—something special to the malt.

The next batch of malt I made was the best to date, with the same color and general look as commercial two row. And the same taste. I was developing consistency. If I could scale up by a factor of two thousand, I might consider going commercial.

By this point, I had about three and half pounds of malt made from the barley I had harvested in Quebec and threshed and winnowed myself. Just a little bit more and I would have enough for the final brew. When I thought about those original projections I'd found of how much beer an acre of barley would yield, it was almost as though they referred to an entirely different plant. I had harvested a twenty-by-thirty-foot patch in Quebec and would ultimately eke out about five pounds of malt. My original field had been about six times larger than that. This would have given me less than thirty pounds of barley. Not even enough for three five-gallon brews. To get the amount I had originally assumed I would harvest would have required a field six times larger than that. To get enough barley to brew the 28,800 bottles of beer that the University of North Dakota promised an acre would require a field about the size of—oh, North Dakota.

WHEN I HAD embarked on my crazy project back in the fall of 2010—or at least started thinking about it—I had felt that I was way out there in left field pretty much all by myself. A one-man lunatic fringe. In April 2012, I came across a link to a story in the *New York Times* on my friend Alan McLeod's A Good Beer Blog. It was about a young guy named Mark VanGlad who lived outside a town called Stamford in the northern edge of the Catskills in New York State. VanGlad, who ran an outfit called Tundra Brewery, brewed beer using barley and hops grown on his parents' farm. That was unusual enough, but what was really cool was that, under New York State law, he could sell his beer at farmers' markets.

I contacted VanGlad shortly after I read this piece with the idea of visiting him to check out his operation. Where he lived wasn't all that far away from where I was. Unfortunately, the demands of growing and brewing, not to mention writing, made it very hard to nail down a date for a visit.

The keg changed all that. Getting the keg shipped to me across the border was going to cost a whack of money, far more than shipping it a similar distance in the United States. As it happens, a friend of ours, Mike Corrigan, is the resident boat builder at the Antique Boat Museum in Clayton, New York. He has the delightful job of restoring and maintaining the museum's collection of venerable wooden skiffs and sleek mahogany launches. I had the keg shipped to him. We could visit VanGlad, and whatever other interesting people we could dream up—there is a lot happening in beer in New York State—then pick up the semi-demi-pin from Mike on the way home. If we spent a couple of days down there, we wouldn't even have to pay duty on it—our personal exemption would cover it on our return.

The keg was supposed to be in Clayton a week or so before we headed south on Halloween. I called Adventures in Homebrewing two days before we left and learned that, thanks to some oversight, they had not ordered it from the mercurial maker in Minnesota. So the order went through again, and the guy I was dealing with told me that it might well make it to Clayton by Friday, when we would be heading back home.

YOU HAVE TO love a state where a gas station chain fills growlers with craft beer on the spot. Canadians used to have a real holier-than-thou attitude toward American beer—it was weak; it was watery; it was flavorless. And although the laws in some parts of the United States lag behind—Mississippi only okayed home brewing in 2010, and it took the Alabama legislature until 2013 to pass a similar law—to visit New York is to enter a brave new world of beer (a beer new world) that many of us can only dream of. I don't think that our first stop, Watertown, would make a list of the continent's more sophisticated destinations, but the Bear World market there, nominally a variety store but in reality a commercial temple of beer, carried at least the same number of European imports as you might find in a good Ontario liquor store and more American craft beer than I had ever seen in my life. They had all the ones you'd expect—Sierra Nevada, Dogfish Head and so on—and beyond that, dozens of others from everywhere in the United States—New Orleans, Erie, Pennsylvania, you name it. They even had a growler club—buy nine of their Bear World growlers and you got another one free.

We spent our first night in Geneva, New York, a tidy town that sits at the north end of Lake Seneca in the Finger Lakes district. This area is the home of the New York State Agricultural Experiment Station. I didn't know this point before I prepped for my trip, but Cornell University, as well as being a pricy Ivy League school, does all the aggy-related outreach for New York State through its extension department. And this station was just one of a number scattered across the state. Geneva is also home to a small liberal arts college. I mention this point only because in my youth I was always amused by those letters in *Penthouse* magazine that began "I attend a small liberal arts college" before going on to detail some astounding sexual escapade. Now I understand—every place in the United States with more than about a thousand people is also home to a small liberal arts college. And I'd guess that at any given moment, a considerable portion of the American populace is attending one. And, I assume, engaging in astounding sexual escapades.

If the Plant Sciences Building at Guelph was a paean to sixties concrete brutalism, the agricultural station in Geneva seemed to have been designed as a tribute to the

U.S. Navy's submarine fleet. Nary a window in sight, and the tiled walls of the corridors were lined with great round dials, which either measured the humidity or gave the station's depth below the surface of the sea. The only thing missing was the occasional ping of a sonar set.

I found Professor Karl Seibert, the man I had come to see, working at an old desk piled high with papers in a small office off his lab. For many years the head of research at Stroh Brewery Company, where he directed a team of biologists and chemists, Siebert styles himself Cornell's "beer guy." When I'd cut through his lab, I'd noticed all sorts of odd-looking equipment. These, I learned, were devices for accurately measuring beer's foaminess, cloudiness and alcohol content. As he showed me around, I realized that the disconcerting open cans of Budweiser scattered here and there on lab tables were in fact the subjects of experiments and not, as I had first assumed, the detritus of a raucous night before. This agricultural station was originally established to help the fruit industry, and later it became involved with wine as that became a big business in this part of the state. Now, beer is coming on. As the beer guy, one of Siebert's newest duties is to give a lecture twice a year on the fundamentals of brewing for a general audience. When he gave this talk for the first time in February 2012, they had initially expected forty people. Interest had been so great they had had to shift to a room that would hold eighty-five, and they still had to turn away dozens of would-be and actual growers, brewers and suppliers.

Local food is big in New York State, as are local wine and beer—the night before at dinner I had a wet-hopped

IPA that, my waitress informed us, was brewed two minutes away from the restaurant we were in. (In wet-hopping, the hops go pretty much straight from the vine into the brewing kettle without drying.) The website for the New York State Brewers Association lists dozens and dozens of craft brewers.

And it was about to get a whole lot better. One of the reasons I had wanted to visit Siebert was to talk to him about New York's new farm brewery law, which the legislature had passed that summer. I had read a very little about it but had no idea what it all meant. Under this new law, Siebert said, if you produce a beer with a minimum of 20 percent of your own hops and 20 percent of your own barley, you get a deal on the excise tax that all brewers must pay the state. In the years to come, Siebert said, the minimum percentages will be progressively increased. The aim is to encourage local production.

Mark VanGlad had already put this idea into practice. From Geneva, Catharine and I headed east and south toward Stamford, New York. Mark's parents have a maple syrup operation, which is something we are very familiar with in the valley. In fact, a lot of the land around where he lives is like the valley, very hilly and heavily treed, though minus that underpinning of Canadian Shield rock that makes our area such a heartbreaking farming proposition. This was a scruffier part of the state than around Geneva—the towns located in the valleys have a slightly more frayed and unpainted appearance, and there are more trailers and mobile homes tucked away in the dips and hollows. Also reminiscent of home.

"I JUST WANTED to see if I could take it to the next level."

The lanky, dark-haired VanGlad said this to me as he and I were leaning over the stainless steel tank that served him as a mash tun. We were in a clean, modern outbuilding that doubled as brewery and workspace for his parents' maple syrup operation. He had lifted the tank's lid to show me the system he used to sparge his brews, an ingenious series of perforated copper tubes that VanGlad himself devised and built to convert what had been a piece of secondhand gear from a defunct dairy operation into a workable piece of brewing equipment.

What VanGlad has done is take the very idea of "the next level" to, well, the next level. Five years before, he had been a senior at Clarkson University in Potsdam, New York, studying supply chain management and entrepreneurship. He and his roommate brewed beer for fun, a way of passing time during the long, cold winters in the northern part of the state.

In the spring of 2011, VanGlad founded Tundra Brewery as a way to combine his education with his love of good beer. For someone from Canada who is accustomed to the seemingly impenetrable thicket of regulations about where and how beer can be sold, this initiative is astounding. In New York, it's simple. "Since I'm a micro," VanGlad explained, "I can sell at farmers' markets. I just fill out an off-premises sales permit. And I need a tasting permit as well, since I give out samples." When he was starting up, he said, "the federal government came by to check out my tanks," officially for tax purposes. He added, "I think that they just checked me out to see that I knew what I was doing." Otherwise the government left him alone.

Tundra was very much a family affair. Ninety percent of the barley VanGlad used was grown in their nearby fields. A hop bed behind the brewing building, planted with Cascade and Brewer's Gold, gave him 20 percent of his hops: the rest he bought from other farmers in New York State. And when it came time to bottle, his parents were roped in to help, as was his girlfriend, who also designed the labels for the beer.

Because of the size of his brew kettle, VanGlad could brew a maximum of two hundred U.S. gallons at a time. A typical batch for him would be five American barrels' worth of beer, 155 U.S. gallons in all. When we visited him at Tundra in early November, he had already made and sold twenty-five batches in 2012.

On a typical Friday night, when the rest of us might be out with friends enjoying a pint, VanGlad would be loading cases of beer into his truck. Then, at three Saturday morning, he and his girlfriend would clamber into the front seat and take off on the three-hour trek to what he refers to simply as "the city." Their first stop would be Union Square in lower Manhattan, home to the largest farmers' market in New York City. VanGlad would drop his girlfriend off there, then head uptown to the smaller market in Inwood, Manhattan's northernmost neighborhood, where he sold Tundra's products. At the end of the day he would pack up, head downtown to pick his girlfriend up and drive home, arriving at around ten at night, nineteen hours after they left. VanGlad sold to a few restaurants and bars in New York City, and he also hit a few local farmers' markets, but the bulk of his sales came from this grueling weekly jaunt. Because New York City's Green Markets, as its farmers' markets are officially referred to, will only let farmers sell in them what they themselves have grown, VanGlad had the Big Apple's beer-swilling locavores to himself. On a good Saturday, they could sell twenty cases of beer. His customers were "beer enthusiasts, people who don't want something that's just manufactured. Sometimes we get a beer snob who tells me what I'm doing wrong," he said. "I never get tired of that," he added with a laugh.

Tundra produced four beers: a woodsy ale featuring maple syrup from the family sugar bush; a red ale using honey from their own hives; Viper India Pale Ale, so named, said VanGlad because "it packs a bite"; and a tasty brown ale. A new gluten-free beer was in the works to take advantage of the sorghum his family had harvested the fall before. In future, he hoped to malt his own barley. When we visited, he had to drive his barley—he was growing six row—three hours to a company in Massachusetts, the only custom maltster in the eastern United States. (I don't know if the crazy schedule got to him, but the last time I heard from Mark, he had decided to give up brewing and focus on the maple syrup side of the business.)

After a night in Oneonta, home of yet another small liberal arts college, we began our trek north to Clayton and then home. I'd been trying to touch base with Mike at the boat museum about my barrel. It hadn't shown up yet, but he had left instructions with the museum's receptionist to give us the barrel when we fetched up there if he wasn't around.

On the way, we made a brief stop in a town called Morrisville, where I paid a visit to another Cornell ag rep, Steve Miller. His job is to field queries from people interested in getting into hops production, and he gets a steady stream of phone calls and e-mails from people who are interested in growing them. Not just from New York State, either. People in Ontario and as far away as New Brunswick contact him, looking for advice. Right now, interest outstrips expertise.

Morrisville is in Madison County, which, Miller said, had once been the heart of the state's hop-growing region. Many of the impressive houses we saw, great wooden Victorians so embellished with gingerbread that they looked like decorated cakes, were paid for by hops. As had been the case in Prince Edward County with barley in the old days, a single season's crop could buy one of those houses back in the 1880s and '90s. Something like a hundred thousand people used to work in the harvest, drawn from the local area and coming out of cities such as Syracuse and even New York itself. Prohibition killed the hops industry, as it did so much of the brewing sector, and with the northwestern states coming to dominate hops growing, it's been a very long time recovering. Today, there are eighty hops growers statewide, though that number is way up from even a few years ago.

One of the biggest challenges in reviving the hops trade is finding workers to pick them. Most people don't want a job that only lasts five weeks. Miller led us from his office on the outskirts of Morrisville to a farm about a mile away to see one possible solution, a hop-picking machine. I had hopes of a machine with long metal fingers that actually picked, but the reality was a little more mundane. You hack down the vines then feed them into this thing—imagine a combine without wheels—on a conveyor belt. Choppers inside hack up the vines, and then somehow, I have no idea how, the leaves and vines go one way and the hops, now shaken loose, tumble down another conveyor belt and pop out the side. Built in Germany, and painted the same gray color as Wehrmacht vehicles in old war movies, it cost $30,000 secondhand.

What intrigued me the most about New York State was the degree to which the government was instigating so many of the changes as a way of helping, well, farmers in the short term, but consumers in the longer run. A farm beer law would be a boost for farmers in any state or province, especially given the growing interest in local products. And it would be a boon to beer drinkers. But will it ever happen? It seems hard to believe. As for selling beer at farmers' markets, it's such a great idea that I can only start to imagine the ways bureaucrats outside the state would try to block it.

I CAME AWAY from New York State with a lot: ideas, impressions, even free beer. But not, alas, with my barrel. It showed up in Clayton early the next week. There it languished while I tried to figure out a way to get it. I really didn't want to make a trip just for it—that was why I had set up all those meetings in the first place. I finally prevailed on a friend's father-in-law, a Texan named Tommy, who lived near Clayton and would be delighted to help. The keg finally made its way across the border in early December. One sleety Sunday not long before Christmas, we drove across town to pick it up.

It was so darned cute. But so small. I figured about ten and a half inches long by eight inches or so in diameter at its widest point. *Baby's first beer barrel,* I thought. I kissed it and cradled it in my arms. I had been told it was from Minnesota, but when I read the brochure that came with it, I was surprised that this bonny wee semi-demi-pin seemed to have been "cooped," for I assume that is what a cooper does, south of the Mason–Dixon Line. In my mind I had created an image of this mercurial Swede deep in the woods of Minnesota, boiling oak staves and yelling things over the phone at the guys in Michigan like "Yoost a minute, you danged wolverine. No one tells Sven Svenson how to make a barrel!" Now I had to replace him in my fantasies with a bearded mountain man in bib overalls.

Following the instructions, I filled my barrel with hot water and dropped in a sterilizing tablet. It was supposed to soak for three days, and in fact, they tell you to never let it dry out. Anyone who has a wooden boat goes through a process like this each spring—it's called "taking up." The wet wood will slowly swell and become absolutely watertight, and, I hoped, airtight as well. Once that was done, everything would be ready for brewing my perfect keg.

MARK VANGLAD'S MAPALE ALE

MARK VANGLAD'S PARENTS have several thousand maple trees on their land and his brewery is set up in their sugar shack, so it would have been more surprising if he hadn't made a beer using maple syrup. Maple syrup is so sweet and cloying that the idea of a beer featuring it seems almost revolting. The reality, however, is something very different. Done properly, by adding the maple syrup at the start, the yeast consumes most of the syrup sugars during fermentation. Having said that, it's possible to make a really awful maple-based beer, and I've had a couple. I assume that this awfulness has been deliberate, the result of trying to make the beer taste just like the stuff you pour on pancakes—maybe by adding maple syrup (or worse, maple flavoring) after fermentation.

Mark's brewing technique is a little different from our usual practice of starting the beer in a primary fermenter, where it generally sits for about a week, then switching it over to a secondary fermenter and only then, when fermentation is done, bottling it and kicking off fermentation again by adding some dextrose so that the bottled beer is a little fizzy. Still, whatever works—although the paths are many, the destination is the same.

GRAIN BILL

3.3 lbs Light malt extract syrup

1 lb Caramel 40 grain malt

16 oz Dark amber maple syrup

(Total 5 lbs 5 oz)

HOPS BILL

2.5 oz Cascade

1 teaspoon of Irish moss

YEAST

Lallemand Danstar

Windsor Ale Dry Yeast

OG: 1.040

FG: 1.009

Method: Steep the caramel 40 grain malt for 30 minutes at 154–160 degrees Fahrenheit, then remove the steeping bag and bring it to a boil. Once it is boiling, add the malt extract syrup, hops and maple syrup. Boil for 45 minutes, adding the Irish moss to the final 10 minutes of boil.

Once the wort is cooled to about 60 degrees Fahrenheit, pitch the yeast and let ferment for about 4 to 5 days. After fermentation, rack the beer off the yeast sediment into a bottling bucket. Boil the priming sugar with 1 cup of water as you're racking the beer, then let the priming sugar cool down. Halfway through the racking, add the priming sugar mixture. Once it is done racking, gently stir the beer to thoroughly mix the solution. Be sure not to aerate the beer at that point. Bottle. After about 2 weeks, the beer should be ready to enjoy.

Ten

FINALLY, THE PERFECT KEG

THE KEG SAT in the middle of the light pine table. Three years before, I had got the idea that it might be fun to get really good at brewing beer. That little oak barrel represented the final step in the process—slightly more than four liters of ale made with ingredients I had either grown, harvested, found or made myself. My so-called perfect keg.

For an audience, I had invited a selection of well-known beer writers and experts. Stephen Beaumont, coeditor of *The World Atlas of Beer;* Jordan St. John, coauthor of *How to Make Your Own Brewskis* and national beer columnist for QMI media; and Steve Cameron, enthusiastic home brewer and author of the *Canadian Book of Beer*. Stephen Beaumont and Steve Cameron had been part of that panel with me at Café C'est What? back in 2010 that had kicked my project off. Jordan had been in the audience. The others, eight guests in all, were food or beer fans, only too happy to show up on a Sunday afternoon to drink and eat.

I liked the idea of returning to the scene of the crime and holding my unveiling at C'est What? I had approached them about it, only to discover that under Ontario's somewhat Byzantine liquor laws, they couldn't serve beer from an unlicensed producer. My little keg could get them in a lot of trouble. Brenda, the events manager, suggested I try finding a brewer willing to fill out the paperwork and provide me with a cover story. When this suggestion proved fruitless, I asked old friends if we could set up instead in their substantial Edwardian house.

As well as the keg, we had brought along a selection of our beers—the Perfect Keg in bottle form, the sole remaining bottle of Pinko, our wild yeast fruit beer, and several bottles of our latest brew, an Ottawa Valley take on a Belgian saison. The food Catharine and I provided reflected the whole local thing that had prompted the search for the perfect keg. Caraway rye made with the same yeast used in the Perfect Keg, locally sourced sirloin tip roast beef and pulled pork from a heritage breed. I'd brought along my tortilla press so that people could make tacos. We had a selection of cheeses. From Ontario there was a ten-year-old cheddar made by prizewinning Maple Dale Cheese along with a couple of semisofts, one made from buffalo milk and the other, cow. We'd brought three Quebec cheeses, all prizewinners: Bleu Bénédictin, made by monks in Saint-Benoît-du-Lac; Bleu d'Elizabeth, a slightly creamier blue; and La Sauvagine, a soft, buttery cheese from Portneuf.

And what cheese offering would be complete without luridly orange Hawkins Cheezies, the pride of Belleville, Ontario, and arguably the world's greatest crunchy cheese snack? Made with real cheddar, by the way. Finally, I'd included a selection of craft beers purchased at Bières du Monde in Aylmer, Quebec. Saisons, pale ales, coffee porters—they represented the most interesting beers being put out by Canada's most daring craft brewers.

Looking at our crowd, I realized that some of them knew a hell of a lot more about beer than I did, even after I had dedicated nearly three years of my life to making it. But the project *demanded* a big finish. Mentally, I saw myself in some great thirties horror movie: standing on a stage in a gaslit lecture hall, somewhere in the Austro-Hungarian Empire. "Gentlemen," I would announce to the gathered worthies, "I have created..." Here I would pause. The tension would build, and then suddenly I would sweep my hand around and gesture to my barrel: "Beer!"

I DON'T KNOW if it was a conscious decision on my part to schedule the brewing of the final, perfect keg for December 22, 2012. In the Mayan calendar, this was Judgment Day plus one, the morning after the world was to have been annihilated by tidal wave, earthquake and volcano, an event that crystal worshippers and pyramidologists from Marin County to Mannheim had been looking forward to with what can only be called unseemly eagerness.

But the world didn't end. Instead, that morning found me preparing to brew my final batch: the perfect keg. After clearing away breakfast, I turned on the wall oven to 350 degrees, poured one and half pounds of barley into a roasting pan and shoved it in. The day before brewing, I had taken the tub of yeast out of the fridge and put it in the hot spot down on the first landing to get it going again.

We had water. Hops. And as of four days before, a barrel. I had my homemade malt, too. And there I also had a problem. I had made more malt in the fall, and based on our previous recipes using industrial malt, I thought I had more than enough for a two-gallon lot. When I had made Wild Thang, the big brown blobs of iodine sitting in the wort steadfastly refused to turn purple, which indicated that not all the starches in my homemade malt were converting to sugars. Perhaps it was because home malting is an imperfect business and I hadn't taken the germination far enough, or I hadn't kilned it quite correctly—there were a lot of possibilities. There are home brewers out there who do their own malting, and from the comments they had posted on various brewing forums, something quickly became clear: if you want to make beer using homemade malt, a good rule of thumb is to double the amount you are going to need. For the two-gallon lot I had planned, that meant seven pounds of homemade malt, not the three and a half or so that would be more typical.

Seven pounds was two more than I had. True, I still had several burlap bags of Mike's barley sitting downstairs in a large mouse-proof plastic tub, but I didn't want to use that. I had promised myself after my crop failed that if I was forced to use someone else's crop, I would at least make the perfect keg with barley I had harvested by hand. Combing the house, tipping out plastic bags, emptying Tupperware tubs and so on, I managed to come up with an additional pound and a half of my personally harvested barley. Rather than give up a week to malting, I decided to roast it. It might not add to the fermentation, but it would give the keg some color and a slightly different flavor than if I used just a single malt. To top out the grain bill, I planned to toss in some of the farm's honey, a gift from our fundamentalist francophone apiarists for the use of the lower field for their hives. The honey was there to give the yeast some relatively straightforward sugars to work with. This was all of it. I had one shot.

And I could not make it work. Over the previous two years, Catharine and I had honed our collective beer-making mojo until we could turn out all-grain recipes pretty uneventfully. This was supposed to be a typical two-gallon lot. When the temperature hit 168, I started adding my malt and my roasted barley. After you do this, the temperature is supposed to stop—and the conversion begin. But my wort would not cool. I turned off the burner. Thirty minutes later, the temperature had dropped perhaps 5 degrees. By constantly turning over the thick mash with a sterilized spoon, I did finally get it down to 155. But it took an additional thirty-five minutes, and who knew how much of those diastolic enzymes I needed had been destroyed? From my experience brewing Wild Thang, I knew I couldn't depend on the iodine test, so there was no way of telling whether I had anything in the wort that the yeast could work with.

In terms of the boil, I did an infusion of Nugget hops at the beginning, followed at the end by some of my Cascade. In the secondary fermentation, I'd add more Cascade as dry-hopping. Before I pitched, I took the gravity: 1.040 or thereabouts. Lower than I had figured. I had obviously had a very uneven conversion. Not really much I could do about that. Homemade barley, wild yeast—in terms of home brewing, I was so far through the looking glass at this point that if my kettle had sprouted wings and flown around the room, I wouldn't have been surprised.

YOU WILL MEET a small unicellular stranger.

That's not the sort of prediction that sends shivers down your spine. But as I had brewed my way progressively toward producing my perfect keg, I started to wonder more and more about the mysterious stranger that had showed up to help me: my yeast.

I knew it worked, but that was all I knew. I assumed it was some variant of *Brettanomyces,* similar to the yeast used to brew sour beers. But I really had no idea how to find out. At one point in the spring of 2012, I had contacted a big commercial yeast company in the United States to see if they could help me, but I never heard back.

I hadn't really been aware of it before, but yeasts are used a certain amount in biomedical research. If you are looking to make discoveries at the cellular level, it is definitely your go-to fungus. The ultimate experimental animal—you can do whatever you want to it and no animal rights organization will picket your lab. It was by tracking down scientific yeast researchers that I came into contact with Dr. Vivien Measday, an associate professor in the University of British Columbia's Wine Research Centre in the Faculty of Land and Food Systems. Some of her work involves using lab yeast as a model system to study retrotransposition—the movement of mobile pieces of DNA in the genome. Some of it involves wine yeast as it connects to the work of the faculty's Wine Research Centre. As it turns out, the lab yeast, wine yeast and standard ale yeast are all the same beast: *Saccharomyces cerevesiae,* known on the street as *S. cerevisiae.*

I first e-mailed Professor Measday in late October about finding out what kind of yeast I had. She e-mailed back saying that one of her previous undergraduate students, Jay Martiniuk, who had worked in her lab, was an expert in this sort of analysis. Unfortunately, he had graduated from UBC and had left her lab to work in his parents' winery, but she might be able to entice him back to Vancouver to do the work or, barring that, get a "protocol" from him to follow that would let her do this analysis.

After that, we lost contact. I went off to New York State, and I really thought no more about her. Then, on a Tuesday in late November, bingo, I had an e-mail from her. Jay was coming into the lab that weekend, if I wanted to have an analysis done. But I had to be quick about it. Typically, they worked with pure strains. When I explained that I didn't have one, just some sitting in the refrigerator in the form of sourdough starter and a tub of dregs I had left over after I'd bottled Wild Thang, Vivien suggested I send the latter. I poured some into a small bottle, cushioned it in Bubble Wrap and fired it off.

In my heart of hearts, I hoped that it turned out to be something really special, *Brettanomyces couttsiensis*, say, though I figured it would be something far more mundane. Unfortunately, Jay Martiniuk could only get bacteria out of the sample I sent. Just too much waste in the lees, I guess. My stranger remained a stranger.

THE DAY AFTER I brewed what was supposed to be the perfect keg, we were off to the farm for Christmas. I'd left the primary fermenter upstairs overnight with the batch in it, and when I went to move it, the air lock started to bubble. That was a good sign. Something was happening. I parked it downstairs by the gas stove. The temperature was low in the house, which I figured would slow the fermentation enough that it wouldn't be done in the primary before I returned. At this point, it looked as though we had done it—despite my qualms during the boil. Made beer absolutely from scratch.

I bottled (and kegged) the beer on January 11, 2013. Five big 500-milliliter glass bottles and the semi-demi-pin. It was a cloudy mixture, and when I gave it a taste, it wasn't really much of anything. For sure, it had fermented, but it was nothing to write home about. But no beer ever really is at this stage. I wondered about the barrel. I use those great old-fashioned beer bottles with the attached porcelain cap, the kind Grolsch comes in, so I knew they would hold the carbonation. The barrel, well...the bung was a small top-shaped piece of wood, which appeared to be covered in rough leather. I imagined this was supposed to guarantee a seal, but I had no idea. Even if it worked, I didn't know how well the barrel would hold carbonation. It was sold as a beer barrel, but I knew full well that a beer barrel has to be beyond tight. This little guy was intended as much to decorate a man cave (indeed, that was one of its suggested uses) as it was to hold a fermenting beverage. The proof, alas, would be in the tasting.

AFTER HE HADN'T been able to analyze that first batch I'd sent him, Jay Martiniuk e-mailed me with a number of ideas about how I might get him a usable sample. If I bottled my beer unfiltered, he said, that might provide him with enough live yeast to work with. I had the bottled version of the perfect keg sitting in our cool downstairs closet. It was still very hazy—he told me to look for that because it meant the yeast in it was still alive. One night in late February, when I was bottling our house beer and I had a lot of sterilized plastic bottles on hand, I popped one of my glass bottles of the final brew and transferred the contents into one of them—I figured it would survive the trip in that better than glass. Then I fired it off to Vancouver by courier.

Not long after, I got an e-mail from Professor Measday telling me that they had got it and she had plated it. But the testing was going to have to wait until May—when Jay moved to Vancouver to work in the lab full time. At the moment, he was working at the family winery in the far south of the Okanagan Valley, about twenty-five minutes from the U.S. border.

On a Friday evening in late May 2013, I got an e-mail from Jay. He had finally had a chance to check out my yeast. Make that yeasts. "Thus far," he wrote, "it looks like you have at least two different species of yeast, and it's likely that one of them isn't the typical *Saccharomyces* beer/wine yeast."

A few days later, I spoke with Jay on the phone. Thanks to an elaborate series of tests, which began, as I understood it, with shaking up the bottle I had sent him, after which he lost me, Jay analyzed ten discrete colonies of yeast in the cultures he made from my beer. One was *Issatchenkia orientalis*, a form of yeast that shows up frequently on the surface of wine in the late stages of fermentation. The other nine were variants of *Saccharomyces*. Six were *Saccharomyces bayanus*, a traditional wine yeast; the remaining three *Saccharomyces* were *cerevisiae* strains, the classic beer yeast. There were at least two distinct strains of each variant. (Jay also explained that these two variants are so close, there is in fact some discussion as to whether they really are separate species at all.) Having a combination of yeasts was not, he said, a bad thing. It created a beer with "more complexity in the flavor profile." Both ferment sugars, but they also produce different chemical compounds that contribute to a beer's flavor and aroma.

Out of curiosity, he had put some of the yeast on plates intended to encourage any non-*Saccharomyces* yeasts to grow, in particular *Brettanomyces* species. There were none in my sample.

Jay had also had several regions of the DNA of these strains of *S. cerevisiae* genotyped and had then compared them with the DNA of common commercial yeasts. He found no matches. Despite that there was, he told me, always a chance that the yeasts he had found had escaped from a brewery or winery. But it was very slight; my yeasts were most likely truly wild. And healthy. "That's a pretty fit batch of yeast you have," he said. "If you keep feeding it, it should go on indefinitely." I had hoped I would get a single magical yeast; instead, it turned out I possessed the monocellular version of *101 Dalmatians.*

IN MY MIND, unveiling the Perfect Keg rolled one of two ways.

There was good: Cheery partygoers clink glasses. Men shake my hand. Women slip their phone numbers into my pocket. But the climax of it all? A beer writer, recognized and renowned, stands before me. I admit, I'm a little put off—I am not used to seeing grown men cry. "My life," he says, his eyes misting with tears, "is complete. After this," he raises the glass of amber fluid in his hand, "I need never drink again. Thank you," he half-whispers, his voice cracking, "thank you." I sigh. This whole business is beginning to get embarrassing.

Or there was bad: *This last one,* I tell myself, *and I'm finished.* I heft the slack form onto my shoulder and make my way down the rain-slick wooden steps into the garden. *Worry about the things you can control.* I'd read that somewhere once. A Robert Parker novel, I think. It turned out I couldn't control the chemical reactions that had taken place inside my so-called perfect keg. Couldn't control, either, the beer's brutal effect on my luckless tasters' central nervous systems. But maybe, just maybe, I could control the fallout. Thank heavens there had been only eight victims. It hadn't taken long to dig the grave in the backyard and would not, now that I have dumped in my final victim, take long to cover it up. It would be two, perhaps three days, before anyone missed them, a day or two after that before the police came looking. By that point, I'd be long gone.

Reality was closer to one than two. No one died—at least not immediately. And if I wasn't hoisted onto the shoulders of a grateful audience, the Perfect Keg had worked. Better in the bottles than in the barrel, I must admit. Thanks to the little barrel, it had gained a vanilla flavor that to me made the beer taste like the love child of an English cask ale and an overoaked Aussie chardonnay. But really, not bad, not bad at all. And happily, the keg had held some of the carbonation.

The bottled version had a very mild wild yeast taste and good color, thanks to the roasted barley. I'd worked so long and so hard for this, and I was in such a fever by the unveiling, that I can scarcely remember what it tasted like. But I think Catharine nailed it. Calling it "a wheat-free saison," she said that it was "mild, not bitter, slightly sour, but not aggressively so, with an interesting dark, toasty note from the roasted barley."

What was most interesting was that when we opened a second bottle at the suggestion of our august beer expert, it tasted different from the first. Neither was skunked, but they had developed differently in the long period that they had sat in the bottle. All my lessons in brewing focused on the idea of consistency—this bottle tastes the same as that bottle, this batch tastes the same as the next batch. Consistency has been the name of brewing for more than two hundred years. With the Perfect Keg, we created something unique—not just unique in itself but in all of its individual manifestations. And we could never create it again. It was as though we had stumbled into some mystical kingdom—Beeri-La or Beeralot—for one brief, shining fluid hour, but having visited, we could never return.

But it had created a legacy. In the spring of 2013, a few months before the tapping of the Perfect Keg, we brewed what we called our Madawaska Saison. This was our take on the Belgian saison—two-row malted barley, some malted wheat, our own Cascade and Nugget hops, crushed coriander seed, mineola orange zest and our wild yeast, which we had been building up for all the months since I used it to make my perfect keg. We'd been drinking it at the farm since midsummer, and everyone who'd tasted it had asked for more. Tangy, herbaceous and only slightly sour, with great mouth feel, we thought it was a wonderful summer beer.

The experts agreed. "As good as any craft brewery," was Jordan St. John's verdict. Stephen Beaumont, who managed to pick out the coriander and citrus flavorings, remarked that it could be hoppier, but as our plants mature (these were second-season hops), this should be easy to do. It was, he said, "definitely something worth developing." And that is precisely what we plan to do—to keep working up our saison. It won't be completely local, but it will be local enough: our unique yeast, our hops, our well water, and maybe next time our own coriander seeds. And it will only get better. I call it S(ais)on of Perfect Keg. And I can foresee many more offspring of our adventure: a rye pale ale with caraway seed from the garden, maybe a new Pinko made with rhubarb and the wild chokecherries that, this year at least, filled the hedgerows. And has anyone tried brewing a fruit beer with haws?

The whole idea had been an incredible gamble. There had been no guarantee it would work. And it's probably good that I really had no idea how complicated it was going to be when I started out. I could have spent the last almost three years of my life on this venture and not been able to make it happen. And I don't think I could have stood other people's reactions if it hadn't—the whole Hi-Ian-how-is-your-crazy-beer-project-going-oh-that's-too-bad-oh-well-I'm-sure-you-learned-a-lot-and-that's-the-important-blah-blah-blah. I had no idea what the brew in the keg would taste like, or whether it would turn out, but I—actually we, Catharine and me, usually watched over by Millie—did it. I wanted to get good at making beer and learn more about it, and I did. I can even fake my way through the beer-tasting spectrum.

The keg itself is sitting downstairs right now. There is still some beer in it. The international beer expert suggested seasoning it by filling it with whiskey. A good idea, I think—especially if I distill it myself.

THE PERFECT KEG

THIS WAS A two-gallon beer, but I haven't bothered with scaling it up. Somehow, I don't think it makes any difference. This beer was so unusual, and so specific to our relatively small corner of the world, that I am presenting this recipe more for the record than in the expectation that anyone will ever make it. Not you, gentle reader, and not me; even if I tried to match it, everything would be different. It represents the versatility of beer—once you have the basics, you can take beer pretty much anywhere you want go. We also created a five-gallon version of this Perfect Keg brew, using commercial two-row barley and malted wheat but still fermented by our wild yeast.

For me, the most interesting flavor wrinkle with my Perfect Keg brew was the keg itself. The bottled version of this beer worked very well, but I thought the kegged version gained a lot of complexity from the oak keg itself.

After the keg is seasoned with whiskey, adding yet another flavor note to the oak's vanilla, I think it might be great for crafting a midpalate, mid-dark ale—or better yet, a barley wine. Ah, the possibilities.

GRAIN BILL

5.5 lbs Home-malted two row
8 oz Home-roasted two row
10 oz Fundamentalist
francophone honey
(Total 6 lbs 10 oz)

HOPS BILL

0.4 oz Nugget (15 minutes)
0.4 oz Cascade
Dry-hop with 0.4 oz of Cascade
in secondary fermenter.

YEAST

Madawaska Magic *Saccharomyces*
Bayanus-Cerevesiae combo
(about 6 oz)

Method: See Dog's Tongue Porter (page 127).

Acknowledgments

THERE WERE TIMES, at my most sniveling and abject self-pitying worst, when I told myself I was alone, pathetically alone, in my quest for the perfect keg. But that was never the case. So many people encouraged me in what sometimes seemed like an insane project and helped me in creating my beer.

For their technical help and the example they set, I want to thank two great brewers, Darren Smith of Lake of Bays Brewing and Edward Koren from the brewery at Black Creek Pioneer Village. I am also grateful to Duane Falk, professor emeritus in the Department of Plant Agriculture at the University of Guelph, and Jay Martiniuk at the University of British Columbia. Thanks also to Professor Vivien Measday of the University of British Columbia's Wine Research Centre in the Faculty of Land and Food

Systems for connecting me with Jay. Although all of them reviewed the manuscript, any remaining errors are my own.

Thank you to the other farm members and "Harold" for enduring my attempts at farming. While I'm in the business of thanking those in the agricultural sector, I must add Tim Wickens and Mike Wilson over on the Quebec side for providing me with the raw ingredients I needed to become a decent brewer after I proved to be a disastrous farmer.

At the born-again Greystone Books, I need to thank Rob Sanders and Nancy Flight, who saw the merit of my idea; Shirarose Wilensky, my editor; and publicist Andrea Damiani. Thanks also to Maureen Nicholson for a superb copy edit.

Thanks to Ian Pearson and Sue Grimbly for the use of their house to unveil the Perfect Keg. And to Stephen Beaumont, Jordan St. John, Steve Cameron and all the others who showed up to drink the Perfect Keg.

I must of course thank Catharine, my wife and brewmistress, for not merely enduring this insanity but actively participating in it.

And finally, a heartfelt thank you to Millie, our faithful canine companion. Our daughter found her on the street in Merida, Mexico, three days before Christmas in 2005, and she became an enthusiastic member of our pack and uncomplaining witness to all manner of human folly. Sadly, just as I was finishing this book, she was diagnosed with a fatal illness, the nasty legacy of a puppyhood spent in the tropics. So a final debt of gratitude must be acknowledged to Dr. Eric de Madron and Dr. Jaime Buchanan, whose compassion and care gave her a few more precious months of life and me the peace of mind to finish this book.